THE TIMBER PRESS GUIDE TO VEGETABLE GARDENING

in the
•MOUNTAIN STATES•

THE TIMBER PRESS GUIDE TO VEGETABLE GARDENING

in the
•MOUNTAIN STATES•

MARY ANN NEWCOMER

Timber Press

Portland · London

For my grandparents,
John D. and Catherine Norton,
my first garden mentors.
And to everyone who loves
to grow their own food.

Chapter opening illustrations by Kate Giambrone and Julianna Johnson
All other illustrations © Julia Sadler

Published in 2014 by Timber Press, Inc.

The Haseltine Building
133 S.W. Second Avenue, Suite 450
Portland, Oregon 97204-3527
timberpress.com

6a Lonsdale Road
London NW6 6RD
timberpress.co.uk

Printed in the United States of America
Book design by Kate Giambrone and Julianna Johnson
Composition and layout by Will Brown

Library of Congress Cataloging-in-Publication Data

Newcomer, Mary Ann
  The Timber Press guide to vegetable gardening in the mountain states/Mary Ann Newcomer.—1st ed.
     p. cm.
  Guide to vegetable gardening in the mountain states. Vegetable gardening in the mountain states.
  Includes bibliographical references and index.
  ISBN 978-1-60469-427-7
1.Vegetable gardening—Rocky Mountains. 2.Vegetable gardening—West (U.S.) 3.Vegetables—Rocky
Mountains. 4.Vegetables—West (U.S.) I. Title. II. Title: Guide to vegetable gardening in the mountain
states. III. Title: Vegetable gardening in the mountain states.
  SB321.5.R6N49 2014
  635.0978–dc23

                                                            2013030867

TABLE OF. CONTENTS

Preface

• •

"The beauty of the vegetable garden lies in more than one of the senses. It feeds the body as well as the soul." —THOREAU

Growing your own food is a remarkable experience. I am fascinated to know that a seed the size of a freckle can produce pounds and pounds of tomatoes. A seed the size of a fingernail can yield a 300-pound pumpkin. A pencil-sized twig will give you baskets and baskets of raspberries! Our geographic region is well known for its stunning scenery, but did you know it's also the home of the famous Walla Walla sweet onions, Idaho's legendary potatoes, and Green River and Hermiston melons? You can grow these mouthwatering vegetables and fruits in your own garden. In fact, you can plan on eating deliciously from your Rocky Mountain garden twelve months of the year.

The edible garden season of the Rocky Mountain west starts slowly in late spring with tender new salad greens, crimson red rhubarb, and luscious fat strawberries. Crisp new peas, scallions, and raspberries are ready for the table mid-season. By late summer, with our long, hot, dry days, home gardeners can sit down to tables overflowing with sweet corn, potatoes, tomatoes, and melons. The region boasts some of the finest growing conditions for abundant harvests of late-season vegetables and fruits. Squash and pumpkins enjoy the dry heat, and can be tucked away for a winter's store.

It takes some forethought and planning to reap these tasty rewards from your garden. You will need to have your "garden game on" in this remarkable part of the country. Its amazing topography of skyscraping peaks and vast sagebrush steppe offers up weather conditions as dramatic as they are variable. The mountain states region (also called "intermountain west") addressed in this guide includes Idaho, Montana, Wyoming, Utah, Colorado, eastern Washington and eastern Oregon, as well as northern Nevada—almost 700,000 square miles. To the north, we've also included 400,000-plus square miles of southern Alberta and southern Saskatchewan because plants and pollinators are not restricted by national boundaries.

Growing seasons can be as short as 60 days in high mountain towns, while "banana belt" areas at lower altitudes can have almost 150 days. Intermountain gardeners deal with lean and mean soils and serious water issues; late frosts and early snows; hot deserts and nippy mountain nights; and lots of grazing creatures with and without spines.

I begin the book with a discussion of what the home gardener needs to know to start and maintain a vegetable garden in the intermountain west. This high and dry region presents unique challenges for the gardener, with its widely varied topography, extreme climates, and surprising ecoregions. And so I explore these issues for you, by state or province, and provide tips on how to accommodate them. Then I guide you through designing your own garden, figuring out what soil type you have and how to work with it, learning about seeds and plants, and choosing what to plant in your area and how to cultivate each selection. By the way, I've included some fruits in the book. Although we refer to eggplants, tomatoes, cucumbers, and peppers as vegetables, in fact they are fruits, since they are the ovaries bearing the seeds for future plants. Annual fruits, such as melons, are a delicious and time-honored tradition in the food garden. Berries, such as raspberries, blackberries, and strawberries are at their very best right after you pick them.

In part 2, I outline a yearlong plan for keeping nutritious, delicious, homegrown food on the table. Each month has a plan of action for creating your own successful garden, with detailed to-do lists, recommended varieties of vegetables and fruits for your particular area, seasonal charts for sowing and harvesting, and tips for getting an early start and extending the growing season as long as possible. Beginning in the short days of January when seed catalogs fill the mailbox, and steadily progressing through the gardener's year, this month-by-month guide helps you grow an abundance of the finest and freshest vegetables, herbs, and fruits.

In part 3, you will find detailed descriptions of the vegetables or fruits that you can grow in your particular location, and listings of exceptional varieties you might select. Each one was chosen for adaptability to our region, productivity, and peak flavor. Included are planting instructions and the number of days until harvest for each particular vegetable or fruit. On pages 156–164 you will also find helpful charts showing approximately when to plant and harvest, depending on where you live.

If you don't have a patch of ground to set aside for an edible garden, no worries. Follow my suggestions for creating raised beds, container gardens, or tucking edibles into borders. Tomatoes climbing upward against a warm fence? Strawberries thriving in fruit crates? Carrots popping up in pots? Of course!

Your garden, your food, your table: Delicious!

Acknowledgments

Growing your own food is truly a labor of love. It's a deeply satisfying feeling to be able to stand in your garden, eating your fill of golden raspberries or bright red tomatoes, both warm from the morning sun. My grandparents started me on this gardening path, and I will always be glad they did. My husband has (for the most part) always humored me and worked alongside or way ahead of me in our garden. And I am lucky that most of my friends, by nature or design, happen to be fond of gardening and even fonder of a great meal produced from the garden. They are my support system.

Being able to share my love of gardening, via this book, with new and seasoned gardeners is a gift. Thanks to the team at Timber Press for making this possible.

GET STARTED

OUR UNIQUE MOUNTAIN STATES REGION

Our part of the planet is picture-postcard beautiful. As states and provinces, we share the backbone of the continent, the Rocky Mountains of the American west. We are indeed surrounded by purple mountain majesties, amber waves of grain, rugged vistas others may only dream of, and a quality of light that makes it all breathtaking. Yet most of the Rocky Mountain west is characterized by one scary word: dry.

A big challenge facing gardeners in the Rocky Mountains is the prospect of persistent drought. Water is like gold in this parched area. Most areas receive less than 12 inches of rain per year. Snowfall—should we be so lucky to have it—makes up 75 percent of our water supply. Changes in our climate and variances in our weather patterns, coupled with significant population increases, put great strain on our water resources. While some areas of this geographic region experience no shortage of water, in most of America west of the 100th meridian, water is scarce and sacred. Some cities and areas of the region have been under extended drought conditions and water restrictions for years. Colorado, in particular, has been dealing with the issue for decades.

There are many biomes, or ecological regions of flora and fauna, that come together in our region: the sagebrush steppe, the Great Basin shrub steppe, the Columbia Plateau, the Snake River Plain, the Wasatch and Uinta montane regions, and, at the eastern edge, prairies and grasslands. Our summers are often hot (90°F and up) for weeks on end. Our winters can be bitter cold, with our land covered with hip-high snowdrifts. Living here—and certainly gardening here—is not for the faint of heart. The soils are lean and mean, often barely supporting vegetation beyond sagebrush and willows. We have caliche and hardpan soils, which act like a rocky bathtub that causes roots to rot, or sandy soils through which any water instantly disappears. There is very little organic matter (humus or leaf mold) to support plant growth. But do not be deterred, my gardening hopefuls. We have what others long for!

We do have long, warm, sunny days that enable us to grow an abundance of sought-after edibles: potatoes of any color, huge squash and pumpkins, juicy corn, mild onions, bountiful tomatoes, and fragrant strawberries. And, with a little bit of planning, and an inexpensive row cover or cold frame, you can outsmart Mother Nature and keep fresh salad greens growing almost year-round.

Following is an overview of our climate and geographical issues and some ways to succeed in spite of them.

Growing Season Profile

Before you plant anything in the ground, gardeners need to know their area's first and last frost dates. You can check with your local extension office for their recommendations, or take a look at the chart on pages 14-15. The frost dates were drawn from the National Climatic Data Center, a part of NOAA. This information is based on average dates over a period of years. Your best bet is to err on the side of caution by planting safely *after* the last frost date and *still* having row covers handy should a late frost or sudden snowstorm occur. Remember, too, plants do best in warm, fertile soil.

Growing Regions

The vast area of the intermountain west—from Alberta to Wyoming—encompasses almost one million square miles of the North American continent. While each state and province of the region has a multitude of diverse growing "ecoregions," elevation and precipitation are the two overriding influences on climate. You will encounter dry high desert (above 4,000 feet), low desert (below 1,000 feet), vast prairies, broad mountain valleys

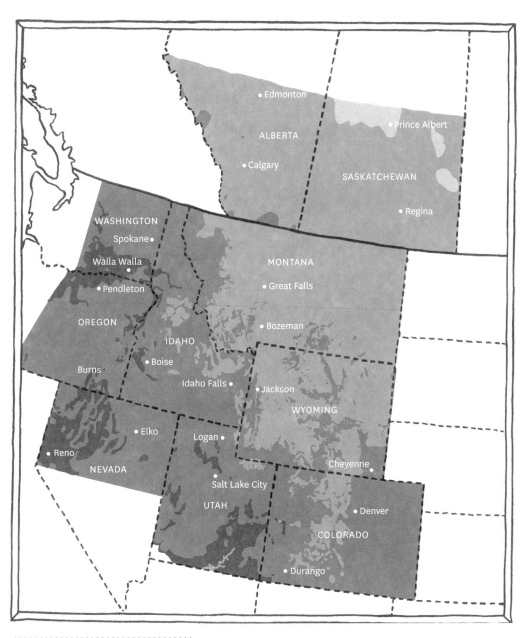

The vast mountain states region encompasses
many plant hardiness zones and ecoregions.

zone 2
zones 3 and 4
zones 5 and 6
zone 7

AVERAGE FROST DATES FOR THE MOUNTAIN STATES REGION

CITY	FIRST FROST	LAST FROST	FROST-FREE DAYS
Alberta (southern), Canada			
Calgary	9/17	5/25	116
Edmonton (airport)	9/8	5/25	107
Lethbridge	9/19	5/17	126
Medicine Hat	9/22	5/15	131
Red Deer	9/19	5/25	119
Colorado			
Boulder	10/7	5/8	152
Denver	10/7	6/2	156
Durango	9/22	6/26	113
Fort Collins	9/29	5/9	143
Grand Junction	10/16	4/28	171
Pueblo	10/8	4/29	162
Idaho			
Idaho Falls	9/17	5/25	115
Moscow	9/26	5/19	118
Orofino	10/5	5/4	154
Riggins	10/20	4/23	180
Salmon	9/20	5/22	120
Sandpoint	9/17	5/21	119
Montana			
Billings	10/4	5/7	150
Bozeman	9/15	5/30	108
Butte	8/26	6/16	71

CITY	FIRST FROST	LAST FROST	FROST-FREE DAYS
Great Falls	9/26	5/17	138
Helena	9/22	5/15	130
Kalispell	9/17	6/20	120
Miles City	9/29	5/5	147
Missoula	9/21	5/23	130
Nevada			
Carson City	9/21	5/28	116
Elko	9/5	6/11	86
Fallon	9/27	5/16	134
Reno	9/27	5/24	125
Winnemucca	9/14	6/11	105
Oregon (eastern)			
Baker City	9/9	6/3	97
Bend	8/29	6/26	65
Burns	9/3	6/21	74
La Grande	9/4	5/27	100
Pendleton	10/4	5/4	153
Ontario	9/29	5/7	145
Saskatchewan (southern), Canada			
Moose Jaw	9/18	5/23	119
Prince Albert	9/16	5/21	119
Regina	9/11	5/24	111
Saskatoon	9/16	5/21	119
Swift Current	9/16	5/23	120

CITY	FIRST FROST	LAST FROST	FROST-FREE DAYS
Utah			
Cedar City	10/5	5/10	148
Logan	9/19	5/23	135
Ogden	10/7	5/13	147
Provo	10/12	5/1	165
Salt Lake City	10/31	4/12	203
Vernal	9/22	5/27	118
Wendover	10/22	4/19	186
Washington (eastern)			
Colville	9/16	5/25	114
Kennewick	10/17	4/14	186
Moses Lake	10/2	5/8	148
Pullman	10/10	5/4	160
Spokane	10/3	5/2	153
Walla Walla	10/13	4/21	174
Wyoming			
Casper	9/22	5/22	123
Cheyenne	9/22	5/25	119
Gillette	9/23	5/20	127
Jackson Hole	8/14	7/8	37
Riverton	9/17	5/22	117
Rock Springs	9/13	5/28	108
Sheridan	9/16	5/23	116

at 4,000 feet, and everything in between. While most of the area is characterized by low annual rainfall, some parts of northern Idaho, northeastern Washington, northwestern Montana, and southwestern Canada do receive 20 inches of rain or more.

The North American Cordillera is the major geological feature of the American west. The Rocky Mountain Range of this cordillera, or group of mountain ranges, stretches from Alaska south through Canada, the United States, and into Mexico. There are dozens of political, geographic, and geologic definitions of this part of the continent, but for our gardening purposes, we will call our region the western mountain states. It includes hundreds of mountain ranges, intermontane basins, and plateaus and is often referred to geologically as basin-and-range country.

"Basin and range" aptly describes our topography: Dramatic mountain ranges dictate our climate. The mountains act as channels, directing winds up and down the valleys. These mountain ranges create a rain-shadow effect, causing rain clouds to lose most of their moisture before crossing over to the leeward side of the peaks. Relentless winds also dry out plants and soil as they blow across the open spaces of our landscape.

Abrupt elevation changes are typical here. You can, in some places, experience a 4,000-foot elevation increase in less than a mile. You may not even notice it, especially if you are in a car and start out at 2,000 feet, but if you have bags of potato chips squirreled away in the back seat, they will expand and—on occasion—burst from the quick change in atmospheric pressure!

Elevation has a significant impact on temperature, precipitation, and local weather conditions. Alpine areas—think Sun Valley and Park City—can experience a 30 to 40°F difference between daytime and nighttime temperatures. Because soils are thin and lean, amendments are critical for successful vegetable gardens. Much of the high valleys of the mountain states will have virtually no growing season for edibles unless you use a greenhouse or other means.

Climate Zones

The U.S. Department of Agriculture and the National Arboretum have established a Plant Hardiness Zone Map, which you can find on the Internet (see the Resources section) and is searchable by zip code. Our mountain states region encompasses zones 3 to 7, from the warmer zone 7 in southern Idaho and western Utah to the colder zone 3 in northern Montana. Our coldest temperatures range from −40°F to a balmy 10°F. Canada also has a hardiness zone map, which is slightly different from the U.S. version (and also available online; see Resources), and the intermountain climate areas of provinces discussed in this book are best described as zones 3 to 5. The zone maps, however, do not take into consideration the influence of humidity or cloud cover, both of which make an enormous difference in gardening. Our high elevations, intense unfiltered sunlight, and arid climate combine to create especially harsh growing conditions for thirsty, tender vegetable plants.

At best, it is difficult to assign climate and temperatures to a region. I recommend that you pay close attention to your regional weather trends. And remember, "Climate is what you expect, weather is what you get."

Microclimates

Within hardiness zones, microclimates can occur across a valley, in a city, and next to your house. Buildings, bodies of water, changes in terrain—think about the foothills near Salt Lake versus the downtown area—all influence the actual temperatures in different parts of your garden. Fences and trees provide shelter from cold winds, while west- and south-facing areas near your house foundation will be exposed and dry but several degrees warmer.

My house sits in the lowest part of the foothills near Boise facing southwest. Plantings near the house on the southwest side have a warm microclimate. As a result, these garden areas are dry. Plants there tend to stay green with signs of life throughout the winter. Crocuses appear first. Daffodils bloom earlier than in any other place on the property. This area is so warm and dry, the winter sunshine and relentless exposure to the elements has caused some damage to the trunks of our espaliered apple trees. On the other hand, the northwest side seldom sees any direct sunlight, and moss grows cheerfully along the pathway. I can watch it snow across the way at Bogus Basin and it will be raining in our garden. I check the local weather report that is closest to my house, as opposed to the typical reporting station at the airport, a mile across the valley and so farther away from the mountains.

Individual States and Provinces

The states and provinces of this region share incredible scenery, mild to wild weather, and vast distances from east to west and north to south. They also have their own quirky weather patterns that have a big influence on your garden. Here's a brief snapshot of each state and province covered in this book.

Alberta (southern)

Average southern Alberta growing days: 120
Zones: 3 to 5

Alberta, with the rugged Continental Divide to the west and rolling prairie to the east, encompasses 255,500 square miles. The elevation drops from more than 12,000 feet in the Canadian Rockies to 3,000 feet at Lethbridge. Most of the population lives in the Calgary-Edmonton corridor, where fertile soil invited farming and ranching. Just north of Montana, Alberta is an enormous province with a multitude of ecoregions: boreal forests, prairies, steppe, and aspen parklands. Much of Alberta lies in the rain shadow of the Rocky Mountains and the Continental Divide, resulting in a dry climate with annual precipitation of 12 to 24 inches. Frequent, frigid, fast-moving winter storms called Alberta "clippers" are well known to residents of the region. And northern Alberta and the northern United States also offer up their "chinooks," unusually warm winds that can be devastating to gardens, with temperatures that vary wildly from below 0 to 50°F in a matter of hours in the middle of winter.

Colorado

Average Colorado growing days:
    Northeast: 140
    Southeast: 160
    Extreme southeastern corner: 180
    Gunnison, Delores, and Colorado River valleys: 220
Zones: 3 to 7

Colorado is the highest state in the union, with an average elevation of 6,800 feet. High plains cover the eastern part of the state, with elevations of 3,300 to 4,000 feet rising toward the Front Range to the west. Summers in the high plains are characterized by hot mornings, often turning cool during afternoon thunderstorms. About 85 percent of Colorado's annual precipitation falls in summer.

The high plateau on the western border has mountains in excess of 10,000 feet. Gardening is possible in the lower valleys of this area, but without a greenhouse or cold frame, you will be hard pressed to grow enough to eat. While greenhouses are generally heated, a cold frame is an unheated simple, small, glass- or plastic-covered garden frame that protects seedlings from extreme cold.

Idaho

Average Idaho growing days:
    Lewiston and immediately surrounding areas: 180
    Central Snake/Lower Payette/Boise/
        Weiser River basins: 150
    Snake River Plain near Pocatello
        and Idaho Falls: 125
    Some high valleys: 0
Zones: 3 to 7

Looking at a map of Idaho reveals that the state's elevation rises from north to south, with the lowest location at the confluence of the Clearwater and Snake Rivers (738 feet) and the highest at Mount Borah in Custer County (12,655 feet). You can almost divide the state in half at Riggins and label the northern part "dry land" (it relies on rainfall only) and the southern part of the state "irrigated," requiring extensive irrigation water for crops. Deep river canyons have long growing seasons, high temperatures, and mild winters. In the summer, areas of the Snake River Plain have wild daily fluctuations in temperature—often as much as 30°F. Yet, the Palouse Prairie is one of the most agriculturally productive wheat regions in the world.

Idaho precipitation patterns are complex. Average valley precipitation is greater in some parts of the state, with large areas of the Clearwater, Payette, and Boise River basins getting 40 to 50 inches or more per year. And yet, large areas in the northeastern valleys, much of the Upper Snake River Plain, the Central plains, and the southwestern valleys receive fewer than 10 inches per year. Low relative humidity throughout the state means dry air and rapid drying of soils and plants.

Montana

Average Montana growing days: 130
Zones: 3 to 6
Montana's elevations are like Mr. Toad's Wild Ride. Elevations range from 1,800 feet near the Idaho-Montana border up to more than 12,800 at Granite Peak near the boundary of Yellowstone National Park, and rolling down to an easy 2,300 feet at Miles City in the eastern part of the state. When you are driving in north-central Montana—big wheat ranching country—the vistas are so broad you would swear you can see the curve of the earth. Summer afternoons are often interrupted by crop-smashing hail storms. Miles City is a hot spot, with summer days averaging near 90°F. Like its neighbor state to the west, Montana has widely variable precipitation. Heron may receive 34 inches per year, whereas Belfry on the Clark Fork River is lucky to get 7 inches.

Nevada (northern)

Average northern Nevada growing days: 80 to 130
Zones: 4 to 7
This book addresses the northern half of Nevada, the part of the state north of Carson City and Reno, which is typically basin-and-range topography with high mountain ranges and wide, flat basins between. Climate can best be described as "near parched," with average summer temperatures near 95°F in Reno. Like many parts of the intermountain region, summer daytime temperatures can swing 30 to 50°F in one 24-hour period. Wind is always an issue, generally starting around 10 a.m., picking up massive amounts of dust, and carrying it across the sagebrush range. Plants must be protected from the drying effects of the wind. The successful gardener will have the garden area soil tested and be ready to amend the planting areas accordingly since Nevada soils are very poor, alkaline, sometimes saline, and poorly drained.

Oregon (eastern)

Average eastern Oregon growing days: 105
Zones: 4 to 7
Eastern Oregon is spread across three ecoregions: the Columbia Plateau, the Blue Mountains, and the Northern Basin and Range. This area is part of the intermountain west because it shares the dry weather and arid, lean soil conditions of the overall region. It lies

entirely east of the Cascade Range and falls within its rain shadow, with between a meager 10 and generous 25 inches of rain and with cold winters. It shares the very low humidity of the rest of the intermountain region. Summer temperatures can be blazing hot, with highs over 100°F, but cool nighttime temperatures shorten the growing season in some areas. While Hermiston and Ontario enjoy almost 155 days in a growing season, Bend may have only 75 to 90.

Saskatchewan (southern)

Average southern Saskatchewan growing days: 118
Zones: 2 to 4
The vast Canadian prairie province of Saskatchewan covers more than 228,000 square miles. The climate of Saskatchewan's southern portion is characterized as semiarid steppe that is subject to prolonged periods of drought. The sunniest of the Canadian provinces, Saskatchewan's summers can be hot and dry, with temperatures of 100°F and southern winds from the Rocky Mountains to the west. Arctic air dictates most of the area's very cold winter weather patterns, but those can be interrupted by warm chinook winds from the west. Most of the rain occurs in June, July, and August (great for gardens), and averages 12 to 18 inches per year. Saskatchewan is famous for its vast grain fields of wheat, canola, flax, peas, lentils, and barley.

Utah

Average Utah growing days: 130 to 150
Zones: 3 to 7
Utah has the highest, only true east-west mountain range on the North American continent: the Uinta Range, consisting primarily of montane forest. This part of Utah receives more than 40 inches of precipitation a year and has snow on the peaks until August. The river valleys, the Great Salt Lake, and the rest of Utah are lucky to get 10 to 12 inches of rain per year. Towns in the lower elevations—Salt Lake City, for instance—have very warm daytime temperatures in the summer, but evenings are generally 10 to 20°F cooler, with light breezes from the Great Salt Lake. Valley edges, at moderate elevations, are great places to plant gardens.

Washington (eastern)

Average eastern Washington growing days: 155
Zones: 4 to 7
Eastern Washington, from the Cascade Range to the Idaho state line, is part of the Columbia Plateau. Some of the area is sagebrush steppe, while other parts are considered grassland with fertile loess soils. The northern part of eastern Washington, near Spokane, receives up to 17 inches of rainfall, with relatively mild weather because it is situated between two mountain ranges, the Cascades and the Rockies. It is also protected from some of the brutal arctic blasts from the north. Near Walla Walla, Prosser, and Pullman, you will find incredibly productive agricultural regions with exceptional wheat and onions.

Wyoming

Average Wyoming growing days:
    Eastern border (below 4,500 feet): 130 to 150
    Eastern border to the foothills: 100 to 130
    Mountainous areas (6,000 to 7,000 feet): 80 to 100
Zones: 3 to 5
The Great Plains meet the Rocky Mountains in Wyoming. The state is home to two of the country's

legendary national parks: Yellowstone and Grand Teton. Its vast, flat, treeless plateaus and basins are broken up by rugged, high mountain ranges and shortgrass prairie. With an average elevation of 4,500 feet, the southeastern corner is considered part of "the High Plains." Much of Wyoming experiences constant winds, and gets little rainfall, only 10 to 20 inches annually. In some places it is cold enough to freeze every night of the year. Great gardens are possible, though, with efficient irrigation systems and row covers.

Phenology: Nature's Calendar

The natural world knows no political or artificial boundaries or calendars. The best indicators of seasons are clues from the natural world around you. Phenology is defined as the study of recurring plant and animal life cycles and stages, especially their timing and relationships with weather and climate. For hundreds of years, farmers, gardeners, and naturalists have carefully observed and followed this system of understanding the natural world. Rising temperatures—specifically rising soil temperatures—signal the beginning of the growing season. Most gardeners in my Boise, Idaho, area follow two time-honored gardening signals from the natural world:

1. Do not prune your roses until the forsythia has bloomed.
2. Do not plant your tomatoes until the snow is off Schaeffer Butte (a high mountain landmark visible across the valley).

You may enjoy participating in the U.S. National Phenology program, a network of volunteers, scientists, federal and state agencies, universities, and others, which you can find on the Internet. You can sign up to record your observations and keep a notebook of phenology events in your garden.

GARDENING
101

The basics of gardening are the same throughout the world. There are four necessary components: sun, soil, water, and seeds. Having a general understanding of how these components work together will make you a better gardener.

Sun

Photosynthesis is the single most important process on the planet. It is the process by which plants use the power of the sun to synthesize (make) food from carbon dioxide and water. The amount of sunlight each plant needs depends on its origins in the natural world and how well it has been adapted for the home garden. Different plants need different amounts of sunlight to flourish. Understanding this can be a bit tricky, so here are some basic guidelines:

- Full sun means six hours or more of full direct sunlight per day. This will be bright, hot sun in our region. It may be spread out throughout the day, say, three hours in the morning and three hours again in the afternoon. It can be significantly more than six hours—in some places you can have fourteen hours of sun a day. Most vegetables and fruits need at least six hours of full, direct sun per day to produce abundantly.
- Partial sun can mean four to six hours of full sun while partial shade often means just two to four hours of sunlight. Included in this category is dappled light, a term describing the light that is filtered through the tree canopy and dots the ground. If you try to grow full sun–loving plants in a spot with too much shade and they fail to flower or set fruit, it is because they get too much shade and not enough sun.
- Full shade means less than two hours of sun per day. Few edibles will produce in these light conditions. Lettuces and a few of the greens can tolerate some shade, but would be much happier with four hours of morning light.

In addition to the number of hours of sunshine available to your plants, you must take into consideration the day length and sun strength where you live and garden. Full sun in Salt Lake City is not the same as full sun in Seattle or Washington, D.C. In the intermountain west, especially at higher altitudes, we are subject to more intense ultraviolet rays from the sun and we seldom have any prevailing cloud cover. Our latitude also plays a huge role in our ability to produce abundant warm-season crops. The longest day of the year in Boise, for example, is 15 hours and 26 minutes long (June 20). The same day in Salt Lake City, because of its latitude, is 20 minutes shorter. At the summer solstice, Edmonton, Alberta, has a day length of 17 hours and 6 minutes. These locations have many long, warm, sunny days, making them extremely friendly growing places for tomatoes, eggplants, and peppers. Another critical contributing factor is our relative lack of humidity. Our dry conditions are harder on our gardens than a "softer" atmosphere—air with high moisture content.

Soil

Good soil is the key to a healthy garden, and likewise is key to healthy and nutritious food provided by that garden. Sadly, most of the soils in our region are lean, meaning they lack organic material. They may also be high in mineral content, and while that sounds great, it is often not conducive to producing healthy plants. Our region's soils were once the floor of an ancient sea, with limestone rocks and ocean sediments. Our region's general lack of vegetation is caused by our dry soil, which is high in mineral salts and does not readily give up water to plant roots. If you take a look around you, in most areas of the intermountain west, you will not see abundant, lush, green foliage. In fact, you're more likely to see sagebrush, bitterbrush, willows, Ponderosa pine, hackberry, and fescue, which are the plants our soils naturally sustain. Does this mean challenges for the home gardener? Yes—but nothing we can't meet.

Two aspects of soil contribute significantly to your garden's success: soil structure or texture, and the acidity or alkalinity of your soil.

Soil types

Soil texture, also referred to as soil structure or "tilth," is determined by the amount of space between the particles in the soil. We have four types of soil textures: clay, sandy/rocky, silt, and loam:

- Clay soils are fine, with little space for water or oxygen. They tend to compact tightly, so they do not drain well, and after being wet, they dry hard as a brick. Idaho's Owyhee Gumbo is an example of this kind of soil. It is also found in Wyoming, Montana, Utah, Nevada, eastern Oregon, eastern Washington, and Colorado.
- Sandy and/or rocky soils are not uncommon in our region. Sometimes we have both clay and sandy soils on the same piece of property. Sandy soils are low in organic matter, but unlike clay soils, they are so porous they cannot hold water. Water moves quickly through sandy soils, taking any existing nutrients with it. Rocky soils are made up of bits of rocks or whole rocks that have yet to be completely weathered or broken down to finer particles. Some plants that grow well in rocky soil have strong root systems and usually require little maintenance.

- Silt is the soil particles that have a texture between sand and clay, and it does a good job of retaining water for root development yet also allows good drainage.
- Loam is the perfect host for good microbes and strong root development, because of its balance of sand, fine soil particles, organic matter, mineral content, and air spaces. It is easy to dig, easy to plant, good at holding water for thirsty plants, and full of needed nutrients. But loam is not common in our region. Microbes are microscopic living organisms that eat organic waste such as grass clippings, dead animals, and leaves and convert them to organic matter called humus. (Not to be confused with hummus, which we make from garbanzo beans.) Loam is often a good host for larger soil creatures like earthworms that grind up and excrete organic bits. An efficient, well-developed soil structure will have all of these components, creating a complex soil web.

Our region has an abundance of clay and sandy soils, but usually not a productive combination. Productive soil for growing edibles contains a suitable combination and size of particles, allowing air and water to circulate and microbes to live happily. Regardless of the soil type you have, a consistent and repeated program of adding organic matter, particularly compost, will help your soil retain water and nutrients and will make it easier to work.

Compost is formed naturally as organic materials break down over time and become part of the soil. We can also make our own compost by means of a compost pile in our yard (see page 131), that will produce man-made "humus," organic matter that is created by combining organic materials such as leaves and yard trimmings in a way that encourages them to decompose much quicker than in nature. During decomposition, the volume of the organic material can be reduced by half.

Soil pH

It has been said that it takes a minimum of 100 years to create 1 inch of healthy topsoil. We may not be able to make topsoil in time to get dinner on the table, but we can supplement our native soils, making them able to support home gardens.

It is important to know the pH of your soil. The pH scale indicates acidity or alkalinity. A soil with a pH number below 7 is acid, while one with a pH above 7 is

DIY SOIL COMPOSITION TEST

Understanding the makeup of your soil will help you decide what amendments are needed to bring it closer to an ideal loam. My sandy soil requires routine, copious applications of compost so it will hold water and provide nutrients for plants.

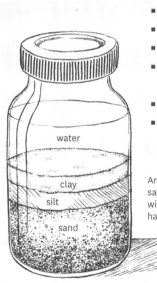

An easy, low-tech soil test with a sample of your soil in a jar of water will tell you what kinds of soils you have and in what proportion.

YOU WILL NEED:

- Trowel
- Soil sample, about 1 cup
- Old sieve or colander
- Straight-sided pint jar, with lid
- Water
- Ruler

1   Dig the soil sample from your intended garden planting area.

2   Sift the soil using an old sieve or colander.

3   Place the sifted soil sample in the pint jar. Add enough water to cover the soil, until the jar is three-quarters full.

4   Cover with the tight-fitting lid and shake well until muddy. Set aside for a couple of days, undisturbed, while the contents settle.

5   You will be able to see distinct soil layers: sand at the bottom, then silt, then clay at the top. The clay will continue to float and the organic matter will be at the very top. Measure the layers with the ruler, compare them, and establish which type of soil is most prevalent in your garden.

alkaline. Soil pH is a big issue for gardeners in the arid west. Most plants love slightly acidic soil, with a pH of 6.0 to 7.0. The soils in our region may have an alkalinity of 7.5 to 9.0, which can cause a "failure to thrive" among many garden plants. In general, some nutrients cannot be efficiently absorbed by plant roots if the soil pH is too high. And yet, if it is too low, nutrients may be taken up too efficiently: The excess cannot be processed fast enough and overloads a plant's system, causing it to languish and die.

To establish your garden's soil pH, I recommend that you do a soil pH test. You can pick up a kit at your local extension office, or check around your area for a reliable soil-testing company. A professionally conducted test with understandable recommendations may cost as little as $35 or as much as $50, and it can easily save you that much and more in labor and soil amendments in one season.

Alkaline soils are predominant in areas which have low annual precipitation and a marked presence of calcium carbonate (lime). There are three practical ways to manage high-pH (alkaline) soils:

- Apply organic matter regularly.
- Apply supplemental sulfur, but only if your pH test indicates that you should.
- Apply ammonia-based fertilizers (a common practice), but only if your soil test shows a need for this.

Acid soils are rarely found in the intermountain west. Do not put fireplace ashes or lime on your garden if you have this type of soil. While this is a common practice in many parts of the country to "sweeten" the soil, it would only increase the pH to unhealthy levels. The best way to reduce alkalinity is to repeatedly add organic matter (compost) to your soil to build it up. Gypsum is often recommended, but it takes enormous amounts and years for it to make a difference in the soil structure. If you live in the river valleys of our region, you may find your soils are, in fact, adequately acidic.

When you get the soil balance just right, you are increasing the odds of a bountiful harvest. If you don't know how your soil stacks up and you can't afford a professional soil test, the single best thing you can do is to apply 2 inches of organic compost to your garden at the beginning of the season and then again at the end of the season and work it in thoroughly.

In the intermountain west, we are especially concerned with having the correct amounts of nitrogen (N), phosphorus (P) and potassium (K) in the soil:

- Nitrogen (N) is used to promote green leafy growth. Too much of it will produce lush, leafy plants with few fruits or flowers. And all that fresh, tender, green growth is very attractive to chomping insects. Too much nitrogen can also interfere with the plant's uptake of other important nutrients, especially calcium.
- Phosphorus (P) is the key to the development of roots, flowers, fruits, and seeds.
- Potassium (K) makes plants stronger overall, improving their hardiness, their resistance to disease, and improving the flavor and color of your edibles.

Calcium, sulfur, and iron may also be of concern because they are lacking or because the N-P-K ratio is out of balance.

Packaged fertilizer will list the product's N-P-K ratio on the label. This ratio represents the percentages of nitrogen, phosphorus, and potassium in the package. Generally, organic fertilizers will have very low numbers, say 3-4-3 or 5-5-5, which tell you the package has 3 percent of nitrogen, 4 percent of phosphorus, and 3 percent of potassium by total weight of the contents of the package. You'll sometimes see specialty fertilizers for growing specific crops, like tomatoes, with high numbers, such as 18-18-21. If you must apply a fertilizer, look for an organic, well-balanced, complete product with the lower numbers.

Water

Water is the new gold in the intermountain west. Water is generally very scarce, and increasing populations cause an increase in demand on our water supplies. Depletion of the aquifers and misuse of surface water are creating tension throughout the region. Water is so scarce in some areas (Colorado in particular) that there are stringent regulations and laws that govern the use of almost every drop that falls from the sky. Yet water is critical to the success of our gardens, so how do we efficiently use what we have and make the most of it?

It is estimated that 40 to 55 percent of all household water is used outside the home. Gardens play a small part in that percentage, but careful use of water in your garden is critical for several reasons. First, water, for most of us, comes with a price. If you are on a municipal metered system, you pay for every cubic foot of water you use. If you are not on a municipal system, you may have a well or are part of a "water irrigation district." With a well, you will pay to run the pump that gets the water from your well to your garden. Water districts provide the cheapest water, but they are not always efficient in delivering it for the home gardener.

There are some options for reducing your water bill and decreasing your garden's dependence on such a precious but necessary natural resource while at the same time delivering life-giving water to your garden for healthy, productive plants.

Harvesting the rain

Rainwater harvesting seems like a natural way to capture and store water falling from the sky. "Not so quick!" say the powers that be. Rainwater harvesting is strictly controlled in our western states. Be sure to check with your state's Department of Water Resources for the latest rules and regulations. For example, in Utah, as of 2010, if you want to harvest rainwater, you must register with the state's water rights department and you are limited to one 2,500-gallon underground tank and two 100-gallon aboveground tanks. In Idaho, you are allowed to capture the rain that falls on your property and store it for later use. Colorado is now allowing some residential rainwater harvesting, while Montana, Nevada, and Wyoming are still developing their policies.

For gardeners in areas where rainwater harvesting is permissible, rain barrels and cisterns can be employed. By positioning a rain barrel directly under your gutter downspout, you can capture free water. However, most rain barrels hold only 55 to 80 gallons of water and are easily filled in a matter of minutes. A typical 900-square-foot suburban roof experiencing just 1 inch of rain will yield 600 gallons of water.

To gather a significant amount of rainfall, you need a container that can hold 500 to 600 gallons of water. You can do this by connecting a dozen 60-gallon barrels or by installing a cistern or water tank. Cisterns and tanks, water troughs, and other holding systems are available at farm and garden supply stores. At this writing, most of the intermountain west has not caught up with the more efficient water harvesting systems available to homeowners in the Southwest. If you can locate a 300-gallon plastic tank and have space for it on your property, you may want to incorporate it into your garden irrigation system.

Ways to water

The best way to water a garden is to water deeply and not often. This method encourages development of deeply growing root systems and strong plants. Plants can die from overwatering as much as they can die from insufficient water. And frequent, light sprinklings are harmful to the garden, because the water is delivered only to the top 1 to 2 inches of soil, which causes shallow root systems and weak plants.

If you have amended your soil to a water-retentive texture and mulched the surface, your garden beds will stay cool and gravity will pull the water and the roots deeper into the soil. When the top 1 to 2 inches of soil have dried out, it is time to soak the garden area. Just poke your finger a couple of inches down into the soil to determine moisture.

Too much water pushes the oxygen from the air pockets between soil particles and will drown your plants. Roots need to breathe. It takes approximately 1 gallon of water to soak 1 square foot of soil to a depth of 4 to 6 inches, the primary root zone of most plants. When watered deeply and thoroughly, and mulched well, good garden soil will retain that moisture for several days.

Hoses. If you invest in a strong, flexible, kink-free, BPA/PVC-free hose, you'll be glad you did. Any hose you purchase should be rated safe for drinking water, since you are going to use it to deliver water to your edibles. Flexible rubber hoses are easy to manage and to coil up when you are finished using them. If you want to make a color statement, you can purchase high-quality hoses in pink, orange, purple, red, and lime green.

If you live in an area where winters can be below freezing and it is recommended that you empty your sprinkler system each fall, drain your hoses and bring them inside to keep them in top condition for seasons to come. Purchase and use quick-connect devices for coupling hoses and disconnecting them.

If you are going to be pulling long hoses around garden beds and vulnerable plants, install hose guides at garden corners. These can be constructed using 2-foot-long pieces of 1-inch-diameter copper tubing or ½-inch-diameter rebar. Insert and pound the pieces into the soil, with at least 1 foot of the tube or rod below the surface so it will stay secure and hold up against the weight of a full, heavy hose. You can epoxy a copper or rubber cap to the top of each hose guide for safety and aesthetics if you like.

Hoses should not be turned on and left to run without your attention. It's easy to forget about them, and then cause flooding of garden beds and wasteful washing away of your valuable soil and seeds/seedlings. And it's a quick way to run up a hefty water bill.

Spray hose nozzles for watering are very useful. They allow you to set them for different applications: the soaker setting is good for deep watering; the hard spray setting is perfect for washing aphids off berry canes; a soft mist is excellent for watering newly planted seeds and seedlings.

SKILL SET

WATER-HARVESTING CULVERT TROUGH PROJECT

Harvesting rainwater is a great way to reduce water bills and a resourceful way to have a ready supply of water for irrigating parched gardens. This simple method redirects the rainfall from your roof down the gutters to a holding tank. Here's how to make the trough. You can find these materials and supplies at your local hardware or feed stores. If you will be accessing the water in winter, you may also want to investigate purchasing a stock tank heater.

Rainwater harvesting for your garden can be accomplished easily with a culvert trough. Gravity is on your side: you simply redirect the roof runoff into the trough.

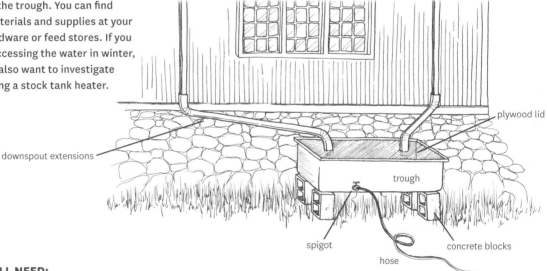

downspout extensions

plywood lid

trough

spigot

hose

concrete blocks

YOU WILL NEED:

- A large, sturdy livestock watering trough (sometimes called a tank, but open on the top), of galvanized metal or durable plastic construction. An 8-by-3-by-2 foot tank holds 320 gallons. The tank may cost about $200. Look for one that has a spigot near the bottom for attaching a garden hose. If not, purchase a spigot.

- A sturdy piece of plywood or metal sheeting cut to size as a lid for the tank with 1 or 2 holes for the downspouts. An adult should be able to lift this lid, but it should be too heavy for children and animals to open it.

- Downspout extensions and joints.
- A garden hose.
- Six concrete blocks or bricks as a base for the tank, for raising and leveling it.

. . . CONTINUED

INSTALLATION (A TWO-PERSON TASK):

1 Position the trough near a gutter downspout, if possible. If not, add extensions to your gutters to direct the flow of rainwater into the trough.

2 The trough should be placed on a level surface and secured so that it will not tip. Position the blocks or bricks (six spaced evenly for a 320-gallon unit) under the trough.

3 If the trough does not have a spigot near the bottom, drill a hole in the tank and install one.

4 Attach the hose to the spigot.

5 Using the downspout extensions and joints, direct the downspouts into the trough, fitting them through the holes in the lid.

6 In areas where mosquitoes can be a problem, add the appropriate amount of "mosquito rings or granules" to the water in the tank. These are effective, nontoxic controls for eradication of mosquito larvae.

7 After it rains, refresh your garden with the harvested water.

Watering cans and buckets. I like to have at least one watering can and bucket on hand. While I can barely lift a 5-gallon bucket of water—they weigh almost 42 pounds—they do come in handy for soaking bare-root berry canes that need a drink before being planting. I also outfit my bucket with a tool belt or tool apron, to make it a multipurpose, garden implement. If you are using a watering can, purchase a lightweight one of good quality with a detachable sprinkling fixture ("rose") on the spout.

Drip systems and sprinklers. Drip systems and micro spray heads are the most efficient way to deliver water to your food garden. These watering systems are easy to install for handy DIYers. Don't scrimp on the most important parts of a drip system; you must have a filter and pressure regulators on the system for it to work effectively. This is a classic example of "doing it right the first time." When installed properly, used with a computer-regulated timer and a good layer of mulch, drip systems with emitters boast a 95 percent efficiency rating for delivering precious, costly water only where it is needed, to the base of your vegetable and fruit plants. Portable drip systems with timers can also be set up to deliver water to your patio containers. If you are uncomfortable installing a system by yourself, ask around for recommendations for knowledgeable, experienced installers. The investment will pay for itself in no time.

Look for a good watering can, one that feels good in your hand, with a fine sprinkler rose head for gentle sprinkling.

One caveat for sprinkler systems. Just because you've installed an "automatic" watering system does not mean you should let it operate on its own month after month. It is very disconcerting to drive down the street and see the sprinklers spewing water during a three-day rainy spell. This can be especially ruinous in a food garden where you are likely to drown plants with too much water. Don't set it and forget it. Keep an eye on the weather and adjust the timers accordingly. And turn on the system periodically, to check that all sprinkler heads are unclogged and working properly. Automatic systems with weather sensors are now being made that will run the system based on rainfall and temperatures.

Organic versus Inorganic

When growing food for your family and perhaps your friends, I recommend using organic methods of gardening, from your soil building processes to your seeds, plants, plant foods, and pest control methods. People often think of fertilizer and garden products as energy drinks for their gardens. But while a sudden burst in productivity as the result of a big shot of inorganic fertilizer may be temporarily thrilling, those pumped-up plants will be more susceptible to aphids and other opportunistic critters and may end up failing. Chemical cocktails do little to contribute to the long-term health and productivity of your growing spaces. A garden that

MULCH ADO ABOUT EVERYTHING

Mulch is a gardener's tool. When applied to the surface of the soil, it will help conserve moisture, cool plants' roots, and discourage weeds. In a garden with a layer of mulch, pesky weeds are easily spotted and quickly removed before they take over. Here are some different kinds of mulch materials:

- Feeding mulch. Organic mulches like compost, fine wood chips, and composted, weed-free manure become part of the new layer of topsoil in your garden and contribute nutrients as they break down. I prefer this kind of mulch over any other, since our native soils tend to be extremely low in organic matter. Money and energy spent on feeding mulches continually add to the general health of soil. For garden walkways, consider using clean, chemical-free grass clippings to keep weeds down. Later, this fine green layer can be turned into the garden beds as a type of compost. Within a year, a 2-inch layer of mulch will be reduced to almost nothing, because it is devoured by the creatures of the soil and garden. We want this to happen, but we must always be replenishing the mulch.

  When applying organic mulch in the spring, wait until the soil temperature has warmed before you apply it, or the soil will be shielded from the sun and will be slow to warm up. This process of adding another inch or two of organic compost or shredded, decomposing leaf mulch to the garden bed is also known as "top dressing." Be sure to shovel it on evenly, keeping the dressing away from the plant stems.

TIP *Six cubic yards of mulch will cover almost 1,000 square feet of garden space (10 by 100 feet) when put down in a 2-inch-thick layer. This heavy layer will decompose volumetrically as invertebrates and microbes consume their way through the mulch.*

- Living mulch. Ground-hugging plants such as creeping thyme, Turkish veronica, and wire vine keep the soil and roots cool, and at the same time help the soil retain moisture.
- Other mulches. There are many types of decorative mulches: tumbled glass, crushed gravel with fines (sand and soil bits), pea gravel, etc. While they do not add to the soil profile, they allow water to filter down into the soil (a good thing) and will keep the pathways clear. In fire-prone areas, use bark mulches with great care; they tend to dry out rapidly and can ignite easily.

begins with native soils, and is amended by organic compost, will give you a growing medium rich in the proper nutrients, a bounty of beneficial microorganisms, and a soil structure that retains moisture without relying on the use anything artificial. And you will be assured that your vegetables will be safe for you to eat and your garden will not be toxic to any creatures.

When pests are a problem, organic gardeners use several control methods:

- A strong spray of plain old water will knock aphids off stems and leaves, if the infestation is mild.
- Insecticidal soap spray, a diluted type of fatty acid, can be very effective on aphids, mealybugs, spider mites, thrips, and whiteflies. It can also be used for caterpillars and leafhoppers; repeated applications may be needed. As a general rule, beneficial insects— bumblebees and parasitic wasps—are not harmed by these soaps.
- *Bacillus thuringiensis* (Bt), which will not harm beneficial insects such as pollinators like honey-bees, is nontoxic to people, pets, and wildlife. It is a spore-forming bacterium that is toxic to many species of insects. It occurs naturally around the world, and is used extensively in organic gardening as a pest control.
- Diatomaceous earth is a nontoxic, safe, effective insecticide. It is made from diatoms, or the fossils of freshwater organisms. Use only diatomaceous earth labeled for garden use. It comes in powder form and can be dusted or brushed onto plants. It is effective against aphids, ants, earwigs, cockroaches, milli-pedes, and centipedes. It is safe for animals, fish, birds, and people.
- Blue or yellow "sticky traps" work well to combat leaf miners, which can make an ugly mess of your beet greens, and also work well for carrot rust fly and aphids, too. They come as 3-by-5-inch pieces of paper, yellow on one side, blue on the reverse, coated with an adhesive that traps the flying insects. Use one sticky trap for every 100 square feet of garden.

Every plot of land has a different soil history. Again, I recommend that a professional soil test be conducted before moving forward with your garden plot. There are just too many variables and events that could have affected your soil. If your home and garden are in a new subdivision, often there is construction detritus remain-ing on your lot. Newly built homes with new cement driveways and patios can leach chemicals into the soil where you were planning to plant your tomatoes. Does your garden sit on top of a former farm or agricultural site? A friend of mine—after much consternation and three years of hard work—discovered that his soils were so inundated with chemical salts from commercial fertilizers; it was not worth his time or money to repair the soil for his own food garden purposes. When I was a beginning gardener, I overfed my plants by piling on the fertilizer until I knocked the nitrogen component out of the ballpark, causing the complete ruination of a year's tomato crop. I had stunning 8-foot tall plants, very few fruits, and the fruits that did develop were ruined by blossom end rot.

Manures from pigs, poultry, rabbits, and sheep can be very hot (high in nitrogen) and can "burn" plants unless they are thoroughly composted before use. If you use them, make sure they are as weed free as possible. It is a sad thing to apply a nice layer of composted manure, only to discover that it is the source of a new crop of weeds in your vegetable garden. For that reason, I also suggest avoiding using hay and straw as mulch.

TYPES OF ORGANIC FERTILIZERS

FERTILIZER	AVAILABLE NUTRIENTS	BEST USE
Alfalfa hay or pellets	Good source of N and K.	Work into the soil spring or fall before planting.
Blood meal	Excellent source of N.	Side dress around leafy vegetables.
Bone meal	Excellent source of P.	Apply where you will plant, working into the soil thoroughly before setting plants in the ground.
Organically sourced compost	Provides much needed organic matter as well as a good source of N, P, and K.	Apply a 2-inch layer to planting beds in spring and fall. Work into the soil as you plant each season.
Fish fertilizers	Good source of micronutrients and very mild. May be high in N.	Apply thin layer of fish powder to the soil in spring and fall, and work into the soil.
Kelp meal	Rich in K and other micronutrients.	Top-dress around plants.
Manure (well composted/ organic)	Variations of N, P, K, depending on source.	Can be dug into vegetable beds in spring and fall. If using pelletized, apply anytime.

Positioning the Garden

If you are starting a garden for the first time, select a spot on your property that receives a minimum of six to eight hours of full sun each day. Remove any existing grass and weeds. Dig the soil to a depth of 12 inches, breaking up clods and removing rocks as you go. As you work the soil the first time, add in compost, as much as 20 percent of the soil volume. You will then have a slightly raised bed of earth and soil that is excellent for drainage; it will settle somewhat by the end of the growing season. Then, rake the surface of the new garden bed smooth, making it ready for sowing seeds.

There are many ways to organize the growing areas of your garden. Different crops do better with different methods of sowing. In part 3 of the book, Edibles A to Z, for various crops, you will find recommended planting depths, spacing information, and instructions for planting in rows, furrows, blocks, and hills.

Seeds

Once upon a time, as part of a botany class experiment, I made and wore a necklace with a green bean seed in a damp cotton ball in a tiny plastic pouch. When that bean started to swell and the root emerged, I was ecstatic! To this day, I stare at my pots of freshly planted tomato seeds, eager to watch as they come forth into the light and grow.

And consider the incredible value of seeds: a $3 package of seeds will yield an entire row of green beans . . . enough to supply a family of four with 80 to 120 pounds of beans in a single garden season! Where once

upon a time, a gardener would save seeds from year to year, today our choices include seeds from large commercial growers, treated seeds, seeds of hybrid plants, locally grown seeds, heirloom seeds, organic seeds, and open-pollinated seeds. Heirloom varieties are prized and sought after for their longstanding history and because they yield gorgeous, delicious fruits and flowers. The Smithsonian describes heirlooms as those in use before 1950. They are open-pollinated types, coming true from seed year after year. If you don't need all of your seeds each year, organize a seed swap to trade with others—a good way to economize.

When to sow

Soil temperature is the best indicator of when it is time to plant. A soil thermometer costs less than $10 and is a useful tool for the home gardener. The thermometer will let you track the varying soil temperatures in the microclimates around your garden plot.

If the soil is too wet, you risk losing the seeds to rot, which happens often with peas, potatoes, and corn. All is not lost: just replant.

How to sow

Depending on the design of your garden, the layout, and what you choose to grow, you have several planting methods available to you. Different methods yield different results, so read on.

Furrows or rows. Many of us grew up with gardens planted in "rows," or shallow trenches in the ground, often no more than 1 inch deep, made with a stick, running the length or width of the garden space. It is helpful to put a stake at each end of the row, with

Sow seeds by different methods, depending on your garden space and types of plants. Clockwise from left: Furrows or planting in rows in long, narrow trenches; block sowing in one large raised bed of soil; broadcast sowing or scattering seeds evenly across a garden area; hills and mounds provide extra warmth and improved drainage for plant roots.

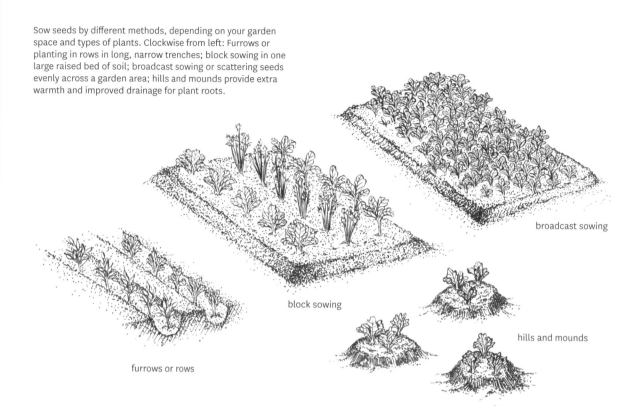

broadcast sowing

block sowing

hills and mounds

furrows or rows

a string drawn between the stakes, to keep the rows straight. Seeds are placed at the bottom of the trench, spaced evenly according to the instructions on the seed packet. Gently backfill the trench, patting the soil in place. By patting firmly, you are helping the seed make contact with the soil and at the same time allowing adequate space for the movement of air and water. So do not stand on or hard pack the soil into place.

Block planting and broadcast sowing. Planting in blocks means using less space, maximizing production, getting fewer weeds, and retaining moisture. Raised beds are a method of block planting. Blocks for planting are often 2 feet by 2 feet square or some variation on this,

up to 4 feet by 8 feet blocks. Planting in blocks makes it easy to harvest a single crop and to replant in the same place after the harvest. Mix the small seeds with a little bit of fine soil, and broadcast the seeds across the block. Read the label for appropriate seed depth. For instance, if the instructions say the seeds should be ½ inch deep, cover the broadcast seeds with a ½-inch layer of fine garden soil and pat it in place. This method is recommended for planting spinach, carrots, beets, onions, and other vegetables that have very small seeds.

Hills and mounds. Using hills and mounds is an ancient, effective method of planting, used primarily for squash, pumpkins, melons, and cucumbers, and other vining plants. This method is especially helpful for these warm-season vegetables because it allows for excellent drainage and increased warmth in the soil for earlier planting.

To create a mound, pull together a rounded pile of compost-enriched soil, usually about 6 inches high and 1 or 2 feet in diameter, depending on the crop. Firm the soil into a flat-topped raised hill, and poke the seeds in at the depth recommended on the seed packet, cover with soil, and gently pat to firm the soil. Transplants do well with this method, since the raised soil is slightly warmer than the surrounding area and the hill has excellent drainage.

Water the newly planted seeds right way, gently sprinkling with the watering can. Check the newly planted areas on a daily basis, keeping the areas moist but not soggy. You may need to sprinkle the seeded areas one or two times a day. Hopefully, you've created the perfect atmosphere for seed growth: fertile soil that is warm and damp, where the seeds will sprout and take root.

Attending to new seedlings

In our region, you may need to carefully attend to newly planted seeds or seedlings. During warm, calm days, they can do well exposed to the bright sun and crisp air, but when frost, pests, or drying winds threaten, you may need to use row covers or other plant protection to shield the tender new plants, especially at night but also during parts of the day when needed. Garden covers can be as simple as old sheets, large paper grocery sacks, plastic cloches, glass cloches, hot caps, Wall o' Water season extenders, sheets of clear plastic, sheets of fleece, plastic milk or soda bottles, horticultural fabric—even a large cardboard box turned upside down. Horticultural fabrics can be purchased at most garden centers; they come in different weights, just like blankets do. Many gardeners in the intermountain west have outdoor hoop houses (see page 70) or cold frames (see page 146), which work like mini greenhouses, for starting seeds or tender transplants early before the soil and air fully warm up.

When you see signs of life where you planted the seeds, and when they have grown a couple of inches, it is time to thin the seedlings according to the package directions. It's difficult to pull out any of your brave, little seedlings, but giving a plant plenty of space to grow will enable it to mature to a productive size. When plants are overcrowded in the vegetable garden, growth is stunted, they compete for sunlight, nutrients, and water, and weak plants are easy pickings for pests and vulnerable to disease.

MAKE IT SNAPPY!

One way to jumpstart the gardening season is to bring home a couple of colorful six packs of 4-inch lettuce plants and other greens. You can find pea starts, corn seedlings . . . even wispy, floppy asparagus starts in little pony packs. I remember the first time I succumbed to this temptation—lettuces and chards only—and cheerfully went about transplanting them into a large handsome container. In about a week's time, they had firmly rooted and were ready for cutting and salad making. And I had gained about 30 days on the season!

GARDEN
PLANNING

When planning your garden, it's appropriate to remind yourself, "The eyes are bigger than the stomach," or, "Don't look at a seed catalog when you are hungry." In January, when you are paying a premium for salad greens grown in a greenhouse or shipped from Chile, it's easy to imagine yourself harvesting and feasting on salad after salad of perfect lettuces, platters of warm, ripe, juicy tomatoes, or a bowl of raspberries and cream. Yes, easy until you are overwhelmed in July by the reality of now prolific zucchini plants. Or how about when all 18 of your tomato plants bear at once? What will you do with all that excess produce? Your neighbors may start hiding from you as you try to give it away.

Choosing Your Garden Size

How big of a garden is enough for you? Gardens take work and attention. If you are new to growing vegetables and fruits, start small and see how it goes the first season. You can grow selected items at home, and purchase some at the market, especially items that take lots of room. You probably have the space and energy to grow several large containers of salad fixin's throughout the garden year, and you can tuck a couple of tomato plants in a sunny spot. You don't have to miss out on fresh, locally grown produce. I support my local organic farmers and buy my fresh corn from them, as well as most of the large amounts of vegetables and fruits I use for preserving. I don't have space in my urban garden to grow enough pickling cucumbers, for example. I purchase 20 pounds a week during canning season, so I'd need vines that stretched through into my neighbors' yards to get that many cucumbers for my pickles.

A ¼-acre garden (10,000 square feet) will feed a family of five for a year. This is a huge garden. If you include potatoes, squash, and melons, you'll need additional space. If your time is limited, then perhaps a garden of 2,500 square feet or even 625 square feet (25 by 25 feet) is a better fit. Some beginning gardeners consider a 10-by-10-foot garden a good size. Plant what you like to eat, but consider planting space-efficient crops: beans, beets, carrots, onions and garlic, and the leafy crops such as Swiss chard, lettuce, and spinach. Squash, both summer and winter, can be grown at the edge of the garden: just encourage the long vines to grow out onto the lawn. Cane berries can be tucked into perennial borders or at the back of a bed against a fence. Tomatoes and eggplants tuck nicely into the perennial border and make up what I call a "bountiful, beautiful border."

To begin planning, I like to get out a sheet of graph paper and a pencil, and lay out the potential garden. Within the full-sun space you've selected for the garden, draw in some raised bed spaces, leaving room for comfortable pathways. A 30-inch pathway will work, a 36-inch path is comfortable, and a 4-foot path will allow you to easily move a wheelbarrow through the garden. Don't forget to allow space for large containers if you plan to use them for additional planting.

Designing Your Garden Space

In the 1980s, there was a penchant for "square-foot gardening," the practice of planning and creating small but intensively planted garden spaces, and those spaces were marked off in square-foot increments. Raised beds or boxes were designed based on a square-foot grid system. The primary benefit of this technique is that all the beds and the plants in them are within easy reach, so the soil is doesn't get compacted because you don't walk on it. Planting closely and intensively also reduces weed growth. And since you are up close and personal with every square foot of the garden, the system allows you to constantly monitor the health of your soil and the plants in it.

If the beds are made tall enough, you can even sit on the edge to work. Beds can be made even taller so they are accessible to folks who cannot bend over to garden.

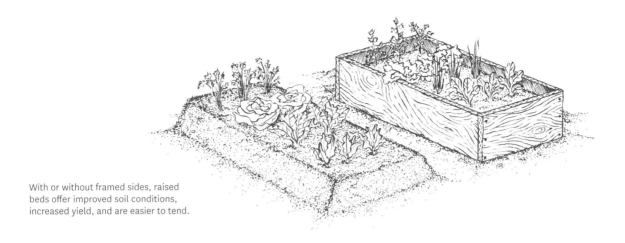

With or without framed sides, raised beds offer improved soil conditions, increased yield, and are easier to tend.

This method is also helpful for determining the amount of space you will need for planting each crop. When you consider the number of plants you plan to grow within the square-foot system, you can create a simple grid for planting the entire garden.

Raised beds are a great way to grow your food in our region. By their very nature they offer improved drainage, which is critical in areas where clay soil is a problem. Also, raising the soil allows it to warm up more quickly in the spring, a major advantage in our frost-prone areas. You can make a raised bed by building a box, or by pulling the soil into a raised bed with a rake.

ESTIMATED SPACE NEEDS FOR ANNUAL CROPS

1 PLANT PER SQ FT.	4 PLANTS PER SQ FT.	9 PLANTS PER SQ FT.	16 PLANTS PER SQ FT.
Broccoli	Basil	Bush beans	Arugula
Cabbage	Chard	Pole beans (staked)	Baby greens
Cauliflower	Corn	Beets	Carrots
Cucumber (staked)	Lettuce	Peas (staked)	Onions
Eggplant	Parsley	Spinach	Radishes
Pepper	Potato		
Tomato (staked)	Strawberry		

SAMPLE FOUR-YEAR CROP ROTATION PLAN

	AREA 1	AREA 2	AREA 3	AREA 4
Year 1	Leaves	Fruits	Roots	Legumes
Year 2	Fruits	Roots	Legumes	Leaves
Year 3	Roots	Legumes	Leaves	Fruits
Year 4	Legumes	Leaves	Fruits	Roots

In countries where arable land is scarce or people garden in tight places—say, in Italy— intensive gardening has been practiced for centuries. It is not uncommon to see an orchard of dwarf fruit and citrus trees underplanted with tomatoes, lettuces, and green beans in a tiny city garden.

When you are laying out the garden space on paper, be sure to leave room for creating a hoop house (see page 70), for cool-weather gardening. Your raised beds can be easily adapted for hoop house growing methods. A hoop house, or poly tunnel or "poly," is simply a tunnel made of plastic or polyethylene over lengths of PVC pipe, usually semicircular and square or elongated in shape, like a tent. The interior heats up because incoming sunlight is captured, raising the temperature for soil and plants, as well as providing wind protection.

In your arugula patch, allow a few aging plants to go to seed, sending up tall spindly stalks that will soon sport tiny flowers. This is called bolting. When the flowers fade, the seeds will mature, burst forth and scatter around the original planting space. These seeds will germinate, and another crop of arugula is on its way!

While bolting is fine in the arugula patch, it is not desirable in other crops, such as beets or lettuces, because it tends to make the vegetables taste bitter. All annual vegetables want to set seed, but the process is often triggered by sudden changes in temperature, especially hot weather. You can slow down the process by sowing varieties that are labeled "slow to bolt," growing the leaf types of lettuce instead of "heading" types, planting lettuce in the shade of taller plants, such as tomatoes, and, making sure the crop has plenty of water.

Crop rotation

When you realize how much vegetation you remove from the garden in the form of harvested foods as well as spent vines and plants, you will get an idea of how much we ask of our soil. Some crops are absolute pigs when it comes to sucking nutrients out of the ground, and it's critical not to tire out our small—or large—garden spaces. Crop rotation is very simple, and essential to the ongoing success of your garden. It will increase the productivity of your garden, deter insects, and help prevent spread of plant diseases. Some crops in the legume family (beans and peas) actually give back to the soil by "fixing" nitrogen, a much needed organic compound. Fixing nitrogen is the process whereby microorganisms capture and transform atmospheric nitrogen into a form of nitrogen that can be readily used by plants. You can see nitrogen nodules on the roots of spent pea plants, for examples.

An easy way to think of dividing up the garden is to remember that there are basically four types of plants in our gardens: roots, fruits, leaves, and legumes. Then, consider carefully within these four categories, giving special consideration to any member of the "nightshade" family: Popular members of the nightshade family are tomatoes, potatoes, eggplants, and peppers—both fruits and roots. These plants and the soil they are planted in may harbor fungal diseases such as early and late blight. If you plant a member of this group in a particular place in the garden, you should wait three more years to plant them there again.

Members of the squash, cucumber, and melon family—all fruits—need special placement from year to year as well. Squash borers will attack not only squash vines but also pumpkins and other vining fruits and vegetables. The squash borer larvae overwinter in the soil. By moving the squash and other vines across the garden, there will be nothing for them to eat. Foiled again!

On the previous page is a simple chart for rotating four types of plants (roots, fruits, leaves, legumes) in your garden over a four-year period.

This age-old system of rotating crops has the beneficial legumes following the heavy-feeding root crops such as beets and turnips. And in turn, the nitrogen that legumes give back to the soil is a major requirement of the green, leafy plants such as lettuce, broccoli, cabbage, and spinach. Root crops break up the soil, making it especially receptive for legumes. Planting in this manner also breaks the life cycle of insects and diseases, which rely on a particular plant family to survive. Come spring, they will move on or die out when their food source is no longer there.

Some plant diseases can survive in the soil for many years. Verticillium wilt, a disease known to infect some types of strawberries, is caused by a soilborne bacteria. The disease infects the roots and spreads through the plant's tissue, causing the plant to become stunted and to wilt. The wilt begins with the outmost more developed leaves while the younger inner leaves often appear healthy but stunted. It's important to avoid planting in that area after any other crop with a history of wilt disease, such as tomato, eggplant, and peppers.

You can mark the affected areas by writing the plant family name on a stake and putting it in the garden where you will plant next year, based on where you planted this year. This simple rotation chart will help you keep track of the recommended four-year planting

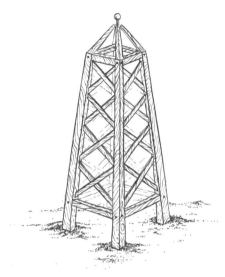

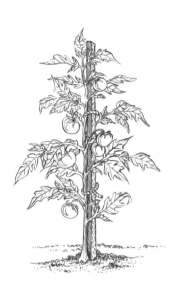

Vertical supports get plants off the soil, into the air, and more exposed to the sun for increased productivity. Tomatoes, cucumbers, peas, pole beans, small melons, and squash do well when trained to grow up.

decorative structure

wooden stakes

plan. You can also make a copy of the chart, include the year you started, and put it in garden notes.

Think About Growing Up

It's all the rage in gardening these days: growing up, that is. It's not about getting plants to merely grow; we are looking for new ways to use every square inch of space for gardening: in containers, up the walls, and between houses. Vertical plantings can be artistic, creative, space-saving solutions for small urban gardens. More than mile-high tomatoes, peas, and pole beans, vertical gardens can include trellis-supported climbing squash, cucumbers, and even watermelons!

You can grow as much food in 4 square feet of space vertically as you can in 24 square feet on the ground. By training plants up arbors, pergolas, poles, netting, and each other, you gain ground space, improve air circulation amidst the foliage, foil the pesky pests, and, in many cases, increase actual yield. Climbing cucumbers grow straight and long, and other vegetables like squash remain unblemished from contact with soil, slugs, and sow bugs.

Give consideration to placement of berries, which can often be tucked into underutilized spots or among perennials. The two most important considerations are sun exposure and good air circulation. Planting your vegetables to grow up on a sturdy support can give them improved air circulation and sunlight, contributing to increased production.

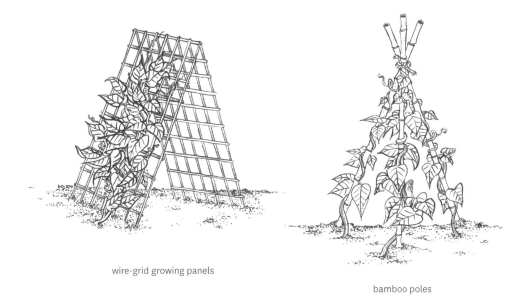

wire-grid growing panels

bamboo poles

Choosing What to Grow

When choosing what to grow, first we know we must have fresh tomatoes and lots of them. And we have family and friends who don't have gardens, so we can share our abundance with them. Herbs are a must in the garden, including six kinds of basil, three kinds of mint (in pots), and two different parsleys. We eat onions and garlic almost every day, as well as salads. We love watermelons, but have failed time and again at growing them. Solution: Buy them at the farmers' market. Snap peas and green beans can be grown up and so take up hardly any space. They can go in perennial borders where their trellises add a decorative touch.

Selecting varieties for Rocky Mountain garden success

Different varieties of fruits and vegetables do better in different areas. If you are gardening in a high mountain valley, you will want as many short-season and early maturing varieties as you can find. In hot desert areas, certain cultivars are better suited to surviving relentless summer heat. Recommended plant varieties are included in part 3, Edibles A to Z. Be sure to get advice from nursery experts on what works best in your area and ask fellow gardeners what works for them. I've included a listing of favorite seed companies in the Resources section of this book.

GET PLANTING

·JANUARY·

A FRESH NEW GARDEN YEAR

Some folks find the January lull after the holiday hubbub a letdown. Others, like me, revel in the quietude of the dark days of winter. It's a time for reflection, inspection, and setting one's sights on the garden year ahead. It is armchair gardening at its finest. Spend this time reveling in the bounty of gardens past and those to be sown. Then, develop a plan for this month.

TO DO THIS MONTH

PLAN

- Purchase a fresh new calendar or garden journal, or start an electronic one.
- Gather the incoming seed catalogs in your garden planning space.
- Make a list of the plants you want to grow.
- Take a thorough inventory of your seeds and garden supplies.
- List what garden supplies and seeds you need to purchase.
- Order any cane berries you want to plant.

PREPARE AND MAINTAIN

- Water (or shovel snow onto) cane berries.
- Check on plants growing undercover and water them.

SOW AND PLANT

EVERYONE

- Plant microgreens in a container on a sunny windowsill.

ZONE 7

- Start seeds indoors for broccoli and Brussels sprouts.

HARVEST

ZONES 3 AND 4

- Without a heated greenhouse, you may not have growing plants.

ZONES 5 TO 7

Plants growing undercover:

- Arugula
- Cabbage
- Carrots
- Chard
- Herbs (hardy ones like oregano, marjoram, thyme)
- Kale
- Lettuce
- Mâche
- Parsnips

Don't forget to check on potential seedlings that may be coming up after being planted undercover last fall. Maybe you tucked a few seeds of spinach in an existing cold frame? Maybe you laid some row cover over a final sowing of Asian greens in anticipation of an early spring? Sometimes just a few degrees of warmth and the slightly longer day length will be cause for exciting discoveries in the garden.

January is for Garden Dreamers

A new garden year ahead, a new calendar, a new plan. While the earth rests under the cover of winter, January is for dreaming of gardens to come. Create the perfect planning-for-planting environment: an oversize chair, footstool, lap blanket, good lamp, and, of course, a view of the garden. In a basket next to the chair, have handy a clipboard, a drawing tablet, several colored markers, pencils, a ruler, and your old garden journals, notes, and calendars from past growing days for reference.

You'll also want plenty of books and garden magazines nearby for inspiration. Delve into articles on kitchen gardens, herb gardens, and small-space gardens. For centuries, households in Mediterranean and Asian countries have created abundant gardens in tiny spaces, growing lettuces, herbs, and green beans underneath neatly trimmed fruit trees. There is any number of ways to make space for edibles in the garden. For instance, we have an heirloom apple tree in a huge ceramic pot. The tree is underplanted with strawberries. Likewise, you can plant lettuce and greens throughout the season under tomato plants. Place peppers and eggplants near the pea trellises, since the peas will be done and the vines removed just when the eggplants and peppers really take off and need room to grow. Don't forget potential growing spaces for edibles in the perennial borders (see the May chapter for more information).

CUT-AND-COME-AGAIN LETTUCES

Several varieties of lettuces are called "cutting" or "cut-and-come-again" lettuces. Once they are up and about 4 inches tall, you can cut them back neatly with clean scissors, leaving a couple inches of green to regrow. Or simply snip off several leaves from the outside of the plant. The plants will happily sprout fresh new leaves. The oakleaf types are especially productive. Harvest regularly, once or twice a week, to keep the salads coming. You can also cut and come again with other greens, like Swiss chard.

What's on Your Wish List?

Make a list of the vegetables, herbs, and fruits you must have and those you think you might have room to grow. On my list will be tomatoes, salad greens, fresh herbs, early green peas, green beans (the pole varieties take up very little space), some flowers, more cane fruits, more strawberries, kale, and we'll try to make room for more potatoes. Sit awhile with a magic marker and sticky notes, going through new seed catalogs. Dream big but realistically. Place all those plants on your drawing. Do they fit?

At the same time, when making your selections, don't be afraid to just say no. Some edibles just don't flourish in every garden in every region. For instance, fava beans need cool weather to succeed, and, while that works in some areas of the country, we go from cool to hot in such a short time frame, favas seldom have a chance to do well here. If you are short on garden space, skip the favas. Corn needs some room to grow. Watermelons, cantaloupes, winter squash, and pumpkins need lots of space to sprawl. You can leave these to your local organic farmers with acreage.

When you are deciding where to plant melons, cucumbers, pumpkins, squash, and berries, remember they will benefit greatly by having pollinator host plants nearby. Host plants provide food and shelter for the larvae of pollinating insets. These plants are visited by the insects and birds that make merry in your garden, distributing pollen among plants, and carrying on their legendary mission. In many urban areas, little natural habitat remains for these creatures. It is essential to entice native bees and their pollinating partners to the garden to ensure success with vegetables and fruits. Certain plants are an important food source for pollinating insects or birds. Study up on this, and add these seeds to your shopping list so you can grow plants that will attract bees, beneficial wasps, moths, and butterfly pollinators:

- allium (flowering onion)
- dill
- fennel
- garlic
- mint
- oregano
- sunflowers

Supply and Demand

Take a thorough inventory of all your garden supplies, particularly seeds. Check their "packed for" dates and conduct a viability test of the leftovers. (See Seed Longevity table on page 62.)

If you like charts and columns, get out an old financial ledger and list the seeds you have and the seeds you want to purchase, making lots of columns for notes, such as "date to maturity," "depth of planting," etc. Thomas Jefferson kept detailed garden diaries that survive today. He organized his vegetable garden into roots, fruits, and leaves, and further divided the "leaves" into sections for their preparation for the table: dressed, salad, or raw. The computer wizards among you will make Excel spreadsheets and databases. Highlight the plants on the list that you have room to grow. Make

WINTER GARDENING TIPS

When the temperatures drop and the snow gets deep, we sometimes forget that there are tasks to be tended to in the garden:

- Water in winter is important. If you are shoveling snow, shovel it up onto cane berries that are near foundations yet under the protection of eaves. These places are notoriously dry in winter. The snow will melt, giving the plants needed moisture. If you don't have snow, you may need to water these plants occasionally in the winter to keep them viable. If you are growing cut-and-come-again salad greens and hardy kale under the protection of row covers, be sure to check on them for adequate soil moisture.
- Grow undercover. Yes, even in January—in some parts of the Rockies—you can have sturdy greens growing under row covers in the garden. While checking those row-covered greens, you may be able to snip fresh leaves as you go.

- Think tiny. Microgreens, planted and placed in the sun on an indoor windowsill, will appease the itchy green thumb many of you are feeling right now. They are wonderful added to a bowl of chowder, on top of a pizza, in place of lettuce on a sandwich, or in an omelet. Microgreens can be grown from the seeds of beets, cabbage, cress, chard, radish, mustard, and kohlrabi. Make a 2-inch layer of sterile, high-quality potting mix in the bottom of a shallow, flat container. A clear plastic clamshell for takeout salads is ideal. Do not use garden soil. Lightly sprinkle the seeds over the soil mix, cover with ⅛ inch of potting mix, and pat lightly. Water very gently, being careful not to disturb the plantings. You can keep the lid closed part of the day. Do not let the soil dry out. Harvest microgreens with small scissors when the second set of leaves—the true leaves—have emerged. Snip them at soil level, rinse, and eat right away. Sow a new batch every couple of weeks.

several lists. If you haven't received seed catalogs, go online, peruse the offerings of garden websites, and ask for a free catalog. If you gardened last season, trot out the seed stash and see what you have, what you need, what you want. Want to try a special new tomato? Can you trade seeds with a friend?

TIP *There is no way I can use an entire packet of seeds and then 25 tomato plants of one variety in my city garden—especially because I want to grow several different varieties. Friends and I make our lists, trade our lists, then decide who is buying what, and share the rest.*

After inventorying your garden supplies, you may find you are short on compost, stakes, or string. Do you need new pairs of gloves? If you need compost delivered in bulk, make a note on the calendar to order it when the snow is gone.

Sunny Days Ahead

Sketch out the garden spaces as you know or remember them to be. Enlarge them as you envision what "they might be." You can do a great deal of this while sitting inside the nice warm house, or you may need to take a quick trip outside with a tape measure and clipboard to check on the correct measurements. Return to the fireside and continue your sketches.

When you have a good rendering of your garden spaces, make several copies and use tracing paper overlays so you can sketch and sketch and not worry about changing your mind. Think of every place you might plant: in the ground, raised beds, oak barrels, old wheelbarrows, galvanized stock tanks, galvanized trash cans, old crates, pallets repurposed into raised boxes, 5-gallon plastic buckets, and colorful plastic tubs. Keep this in mind: A shrub-type or large vegetable plant—tomato, potato, cucumber—needs just 5 gallons of soil in which to grow successfully.

Remember, too, that while most vegetables and fruits need full sun to flourish, some edibles can get by with a little less than full sun. In the heat of the summer, lettuce and basil will benefit from intercropping and being planted under taller plants. Try to envision where you will be able to add second plantings and underplantings of edibles as the summer progresses.

When you have the lists sorted out, place the seed orders as soon as possible. If this is the year you add cane berries, order bare-root varieties now for delivery in late February or early March.

SKILL SET

SEEDS OF LIFE AND THE LIFE OF SEEDS

Seeds are miraculous—like little tiny computer chips before there were computer chips. They are encoded with the secrets of the garden universe and have the capability, if stored properly, of providing food and nourishment to all of mankind. No small task. Seeds should be saved and stored under three critical conditions: cool (less than 50°F), dark, and dry (less than 40 percent humidity). Seeds have expiration dates (viability rates) on the package, and you can increase the probability of their success by following a few guidelines and testing your seeds for viability each year.

There are many alternatives to growing transplantable plants from seed. Check with your local farmers' market, find a CSA (Community Supported Agriculture) farm or farmer, or buy seedlings from a reputable locally owned nursery. One of my local CSA farms has an annual tomato and pepper seedling sale. They offer 84 varieties of tomatoes and 36 types of peppers. I love that kind of selection. Mark the sale date on the calendar and plan to get in line.

SEED LONGEVITY

1 TO 2 YEARS	3 TO 4 YEARS	5 TO 6 YEARS
Corn	Beans	Cucumbers
Leeks	Beets	Lettuce
Onions	Cabbage	Melons
Parsley	family plants	Spinach
Peppers	Carrots	
	Eggplant	
	Peas	
	Pumpkins	
	Squash	
	Tomatoes	

(average, if stored properly)

BABY, IT'S COLD OUTSIDE

It's a really good thing we have some down time in our neck of the woods. Hopefully, winter's blanket of snow has gently covered your garden, and plentifully packed it on the local ski hill. It's still entirely too cold here— in most places the ground is still frozen—to plant anything but microgreens on the sunny windowsill. There is plenty of time to seek inspiration from dozens of resources and create that bountiful garden on paper.

TO DO THIS MONTH

PLAN

- Take in a garden show.
- Order bare-root berries and fruit canes, if you haven't done so already.
- Order organic seed potatoes and onion sets.
- Test seeds in your inventory for viability.
- Place orders for new seeds.
- Sign up for gardening classes (planting and pruning classes fill up quickly).

PREPARE AND MAINTAIN

EVERYONE

- Gather supplies for seed starting: heat mats, soil mix, grow lights.

ZONES 3 AND 4

- Gather supplies for building a cold frame (see page 146) or hoop house (see page 70) now, so building can begin when the ground thaws.

ZONES 5 TO 7

- Set up a cold frame for next month.

TO DO THIS MONTH ...CONTINUED

SOW AND PLANT

EVERYONE

Several hardy herbs can be started now, indoors:

- Lavender
- Marjoram
- Plant more microgreens.
- Check on under-cover greens for adequate moisture.
- Oregano
- Rosemary
- Thyme

ZONE 7

- Start seeds indoors for broccoli, Brussels sprouts, cabbage, eggplants, and peppers.

HARVEST

- Arugula
- Cabbage
- Chard
- Chives
- Garlic
- Herbs (hardy ones like oregano, marjoram, thyme)
- Kale
- Mâche
- Microgreens

If you are home by the fire, enjoy a cup of hot tea with scones and preserves, preferably preserves you made yourself from last season's garden. Make a note of the various flavors of small-batch preserves you'd like to put by for next winter. Use up the last frozen and preserved herb pestos, vegetables, and fruits. To warm the house with smells of summer, make a roast and season it with herbs you dried from the garden.

Planning and More Planning

It's hard to sit inside when you have so many big plans for the growing season ahead. We all have a slight case of cabin fever by February. If you don't ski, knit, or spend the month at a tropical island paradise, what else is there to do but plan a garden?

Take in a garden show. Traditionally, garden shows are held in early spring. There are local shows and then there are the biggies. The Northwest Flower and Garden Show in Seattle is the nation's second largest. There are shows in Portland, Salt Lake, Bozeman, San Francisco, Denver, and Boise. This is where great ideas are born and stolen. Yes, stolen. The designers of these gardens fully expect you to take their best ideas home and try them out in your garden. Go armed with a notebook and camera. Ask lots of questions. Buy good vegetable seeds from the vendors. Seek advice from the folks selling berries. Check out local gardening classes, which are offered by the hundreds, taught by hobbyists and experts alike. Local nurseries and Master Gardener programs will have classes on everything from growing tomatoes to raising chickens.

Even though we may still have snow on the ground, it's getting late to order your bare-root fruit canes. The very best varieties get snapped up early. Don't worry; they won't ship until it's time to plant in your area.

Start some microgreens by scattering a small amount of seed mix among the existing plantings on your windowsill. You can let some greens get a little taller depending on how hungry you are and how many trays you planted. And sow some herbs. They can be grown from seed or, in the case of rosemary, from cuttings.

Share and swap seeds with fellow gardeners in plenty of time for starting indoors. In preparation for seed starting, make sure the planting trays are clean: wash them in warm, soapy water, rinse, and dry them thoroughly. Check the quantity of planting mix on hand. If you are planning to use grow lights, see that they are in good working order. A "grow light" is a special light bulb for growing plants indoors. This artificial light source stimulates plant growth by emitting an electromagnetic spectrum needed for photosynthesis and plant development. Are you going to need warming mats for your seed-starting operation? Heating mats, or grow mats, are electric mats that provide a uniform radiant heat for quick propagation of your seedlings. Order those as well.

And what about the seeds you have on hand? Were they stored under optimal conditions? Or, like me, did you toss the envelopes in a drawer to be dealt with next year? Well, now is next year. The bigger question is, are they still alive?

Seeds have a shelf life. It is easy to determine their viability by checking their rate of germination with a very simple test. From each package of seeds, select ten. Take a paper towel, fold it in half, and dampen it. Now, open it and place the ten seeds on one of the halves.

Space them out evenly, giving them room to sprout. Fold the other half over them to cover them. Put this paper towel in a sealed plastic bag with a clear label indicating the seed type, name, and date of the test, and put it somewhere warm to germinate. Every day check for moistness, spritzing if necessary to keep the towel damp but not soggy. Within a few days, the seeds should start to germinate, or sprout. The seed packet will tell you how long you can expect to wait for a particular type of seed to germinate. Lettuce, for example, will take seven to ten days. Within three to four days of the first one sprouting, the rest should have shown signs of life as well. If seven out of the ten seeds germinate, you have a 70 percent rate. If only five of ten sprout, you have a 50 percent rate. If you are determined to use the seeds with the 50 percent rate, know that you should sow those seeds twice as thick to get a full row of the desired vegetable.

Seed Packet Information

Whether you are making packets for your own saved seeds or purchasing seeds already packaged, informative

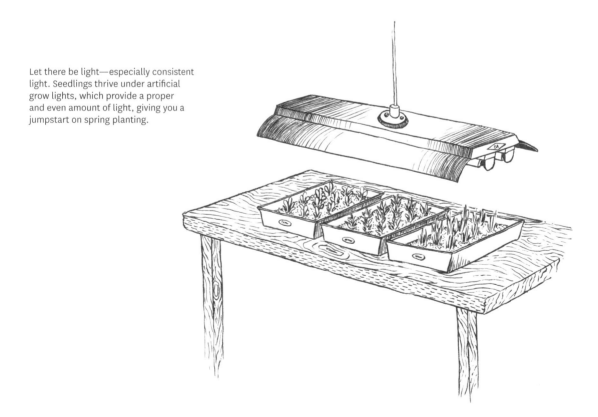

Let there be light—especially consistent light. Seedlings thrive under artificial grow lights, which provide a proper and even amount of light, giving you a jumpstart on spring planting.

packages are extremely helpful when it comes to sowing a garden. A useful packet should have most of the following information:

- Common name of the vegetable or fruit
- Botanical name
- Words or stamp indicating whether the seeds are non-GMO/hybrid (F1), and if the variety is an heirloom variety. (A GMO, or genetically modified organism, is the result of a laboratory process where genes from the DNA of one species are extracted and artificially forced into the genes of an unrelated plant or animal. The foreign genes may come from bacteria, viruses, insects, animals, or even humans. Hybrid, or F1, is the first-generation cross between two different plants.)
- A clear picture and/or good description of the vegetable or fruit
- Days from planting time to maturity
- When to sow: "after the last chance of spring frost," or "in early spring as soon as the soil can be worked"
- Days until germination
- Seed spacing
- Thinning guidance
- When to start indoors (if applicable)
- Approximately how many plants you can expect to grow from the seeds inside (for instance, "this packet plants 2 to 3 mounds")

All About Love Apples

As you contemplate the seeds you will sow for the season, give some special thought to tomatoes, which is probably the most popular plant in the home garden.

The once-feared "love apple" has many shapes, colors, plant heights, admirers, and controversies surrounding it. One of my favorite local nurseries carries 130 different varieties. Entire books and catalogs are devoted to growing tomatoes. As you work your way through the seed catalogs, here's a quick reminder of the basic types:

- Heirloom: plants grown and preserved for generations because of their exceptional flavor, color, hardiness, and particular characteristics that make them valuable in their home region.
- Hybrid: varieties that have been crossbred, generally for improved disease resistance and uniform shape. Hybrids seldom have the flavor of heirlooms.
- Cherry and grape: small, intensely flavored fruits borne in clusters, usually early to produce and perfect for small gardens.
- Beefsteak: large tomatoes often weighing as much as a pound or more each, and needing a long growing season. Several heirloom cultivars, while not as uniform in shape as the hybrids, surpass them in flavor.
- Paste: generally elongated in shape, these are dense and meaty, and not as juicy. They have a pronounced tomato flavor, making them well suited for sauce making, canning, salsa, and sun-dried tomatoes.
- Grafted tomatoes: relatively new on the market, they are purported to do well in short-season, cooler growing regions. Plant these exactly as they come in the pot, not deeper, since they are grafted.
- Dwarf: the newest of the new, only reaching 4 feet in height, perfectly suited for patio pots. These are supposed to have a rich flavor and will bear fruit throughout the growing season.

BUILDING A HOOP HOUSE

A hoop house can be quickly assembled in the garden. Stake off the space you want to enclose. A good starting point is to create a garden space or boxed-in raised bed 3 feet wide by 6 feet long. The round plastic clips can be found at a nursery, and jumbo owl clips are available at an office supply store.

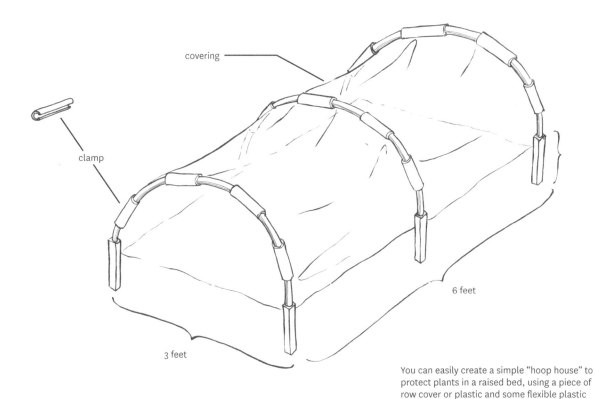

covering

clamp

3 feet

6 feet

You can easily create a simple "hoop house" to protect plants in a raised bed, using a piece of row cover or plastic and some flexible plastic piping and clamps.

YOU WILL NEED:

- 6 rebar stakes, 18 inches long and ¼ inch diameter
- Hammer or mallet for pounding stakes

- Three 6-foot lengths of ¾-inch-diameter flexible plastic pipe
- 1 piece of floating row cover of heavy clear or opaque plastic, 12 by 8 feet

- 12 round plastic clips or jumbo owl clips (for holding row cover in place on the hoops)
- 6 to 8 bricks or heavy stones

STEPS:

1   Clear the space for the hoop house garden bed. The soil should be well prepared for planting, since this bed will be used as part of the garden when the weather warms up.

2   Pound in a rebar stake at each corner, and pound 1 stake midway down each side of the bed.

3   Position the lengths of flexible pipe, or "hoops," in an arc by placing one open end over one rebar stake and the other end over the opposite rebar stake. Repeat, with the other two pairs of stakes.

4   To attach the row cover, drape it over the hoops and use the round plastic clips or the owl clips to clamp it into place.

5   Position the bricks to keep the end pieces down.

6   Lift the row cover to tend to plantings. Be careful on sunny days: even a lightweight row cover can cause the area within to reach very high temperatures.

Alternative: A similar but smaller enclosure—called a cold frame—can be easily made by creating a box and by covering it with an old framed window (see page 146).

·MARCH·

GO PLAY
IN THE DIRT

As someone once said, "Now is the time and this is the place." That sums up the month of March for gardeners. Come mid-March, right around St. Patrick's Day, the gardener's world starts to speed up. The knobby red, gnarled leaves of the rhubarb are just starting to unfurl and there are signs of green life poking up in the garden. For the head gardener of the edible garden, it's time to get a move on.

TO DO THIS MONTH

PLAN

- Review last year's garden journal.
- Make good weather notes.
- Attend as many garden shows as you can.
- Keep row covers or protective plastic sheets handy.

PREPARE AND MAINTAIN

EVERYONE

- Begin preparation of garden soil.

ZONES 5 TO 7

- Prune cane fruit (blackberries and raspberries).
- Test and repair automated irrigation system, hoses, and timers.
- Check new growth on hardy, established herbs, and prune if not too early.

SOW AND PLANT

ZONES 3 AND 4

- Start indoors: broccoli, Brussels sprouts, cabbage, cauliflower, collards, eggplants, onions (bulb).

ZONES 5 AND 6

- Start indoors: broccoli, Brussels sprouts, cabbage, cauliflower, collards, eggplants, kale, kohlrabi, onions (green), onions (bulb), parsnips, peppers, and tomatoes.
- Purchase and plant fresh starts/crowns/canes of rhubarb, strawberries, cane berries, blueberries, asparagus.
- Start indoors: tomatoes, peppers, eggplants, and tomatillos, last half of the month.

ZONE 7

- Start tomatoes indoors, first half of the month.

HARVEST

- Arugula
- Herbs (hardy ones like oregano, rosemary, and thyme)
- Lettuce (cut-and-come-again varieties' tender new growth)
- Parsley

So Much To Do, So Little Time

Note in your journal all the wild weather swings at this time of year in your area. It's fun to keep track, and the notes become very helpful next year when you are making decisions. If the soil is workable (warm and dry), prepare it and set out rhubarb, kohlrabi, strawberries, and cane berries. Have copious amounts of rich, aged, organic compost on hand for the planting. Follow the instructions in Edibles A to Z for each variety.

If you have hardy herbs that are showing new growth and you are in the coldest parts of the intermountain west, go ahead and prune them. Give them a good haircut, and remove any dead twigs, branches, or "duff" where earwigs, sow bugs, and slugs tend to hide.

In the mountain states, peas and potatoes are often planted on St. Patrick's Day, March 17, if the soil is workable. Onions, radishes, carrots, endive, beets, parsnips, chard, turnips, cauliflower, broccoli, cabbage, and asparagus can go in now as well. Directly sow Asian greens, arugula, cut-and-come-again lettuces, and remove the row cover from the overwintered crop.

Chit your spuds. Also called "greensprouting" but not nearly as much fun to say or do as chitting, it means getting your potatoes to sprout before you put them in the soil. In our region, it's an excellent way to jumpstart the potato plant's growth. Here's how: Purchase organic potatoes or organic seed potatoes. Put them in a dark, warm (room-temperature) place for at least one week. Then, move them to a cooler part of the house or garage, with good light, where the temperature is about 50°F. You will soon see strong sprouts appear and the potatoes will be ready to plant. Plant each "chitted" potato as a whole, or cut into pieces, each having at least 2 good sprouts or "eyes."

Making Your Bed

Remember those carefully drafted plans you made in January? On the first warmish day, gather them up, get a string, some stakes, and a tape measure, and head outside. Stake off the areas as you drew them on paper. Remember, the garden will do best with a full day of sunlight. Will the areas you've staked out work? Using rocks or sticks, establish positions for the tomatoes you will be planting later in May, in the perennial border or wherever they work best. How many tomato stakes and pea trellises will you need? Mark their positions. Determine where the potatoes will be hilled up. Did you want an asparagus bed? Is there room for rhubarb? This is the time to ask these questions.

Now is also the time to determine how many containers and planting boxes you are going to need. Does every seed, seedling, or fruit plant have a home to grow into? If not, you've joined the ranks of legions of fellow gardeners who dream of gardens they could never manage. We all seem to have this crazy idea our gardens can accommodate enough plants to support a farmers' market. But we must have a plan and use it. Don't forget, you can underplant tomatoes with basil and lettuce, too. That will give you a few extra square feet of planting space. Can you go vertical? Grow those cucumbers up a trellis? Is there a fence handy? For narrow spaces, look for pole beans, climbing varieties of everything, and consider indeterminate tomatoes. Indeterminate

For planting strawberries in the home garden, the best method is to plant them at the proper depth in spaced rows. (a) In year 1, set out the plants, 18 to 24 inches apart in each direction. (b) As they grow, each mother plant will send out runners with "daughter" plants at the end. In year 2, keep only four daughters, radiated out from the mother at equal distance. In year 3, remove the mother plant.

a

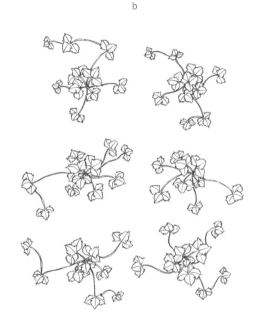

b

18–24 inches

18–24 inches

tomatoes are those cultivars that produce until a killing frost and grow quite tall. Strawberries can be edging plants in flowerbeds or along pathways.

Now that the soil is workable, it's time to make new garden spaces. If you have existing beds, freshen them by loosening any soil clumps and adding compost if needed. You've staked out the space, now create the actual garden. Raised beds are a gardener's dream. The elevated planting spaces create good drainage, and

anything "raised" to be closer to the gardener is easier on the back muscles.

Strawberries, crowns of rhubarb and asparagus, as well as all kinds of cane fruits start showing up in the nurseries this month. If you can work the soil—perhaps you just created a new garden space—you can get these in the ground. If you are going to try raising blueberries, buy early when the selection is the best.

Garden shows are still being staged this month in

towns near you. Plan to attend, and pick up coupons for thrifty discounts and free products at your local nurseries. Sit in on some classes and observe gardening demos. Check out the new supplies and latest varieties of plants.

Every now and again, the weather can turn fierce and wintry. In fact, you should expect it to do this in our region. Know where your garden row covers are, and be able to grab them and use them at a moment's notice.

SKILL SET

MAKING A GARDEN

RAISED BEDS

Making a new garden bed is a bit of work but yields great payoff for years to come. Select the site. First, it should have good drainage with no standing water or mushy areas. Second, the site should have at least six hours of sun per day. This may take some thought, especially in March, since the sun will be in a different position in the most important growing months. Generally, a south-, southeast-, or southwest-facing area is a good choice.

1 Stake out the area to be dug, if you haven't already.

2 Have a large tarp, pointed shovel, and gloves at hand.

3 If sod covers the space, you will need to remove it. If you are creating a large garden, rent a sod cutter to make the job easier. Cut down through the sod, working in small areas at a time. Run the shovel under the roots, and remove the sod to the tarp. These sod pieces can be used to make lawn repairs in other areas. Or, add them to the compost pile.

4 Once the sod has been removed, you should be working about 3 inches or so below the original soil level. Remove the topsoil—the next 4 to 6 inches of soil—and place it on the tarp. Break up clumps of earth and remove rocks. Go as deep as you can dig or have it rototilled (advisable for the first season only). If you have had a soil test, now is the time to add the recommended amendments. If you skipped the test, add at least ¼ to ⅓ as much aged, organic compost as soil. Mix it thoroughly with the topsoil you've set aside and place the amended soil back in the planting area. The soil level will be a bit higher than when you started because of the addition of the compost.

5 If at this point you run into hardpan or clay, you will have to remove it with a pick or it will prevent drainage. It is critical to make the garden a space that drains well.

Water this area thoroughly. Let it rest a day before planting.

AN ALTERNATIVE METHOD

Layered or lasagna gardening is an easy way to create a new garden space, especially if you have a few months to let the bed rest after setting it up.

1 Stake out the area to be turned into a garden bed. Remove weeds. You may leave the sod in place. Cover the space with six to eight layers of newspaper. Wet this paper thoroughly.

2 Use a good soil (purchased, if necessary) or create soil using 50 percent topsoil and 50 percent aged organic compost. These products should come from a very reliable source. Cheaper is not better. You don't want cheaper, weedy soil that someone is trying to get rid of. Ask friends for recommendations for the best soil sources. You want to create a 6 to 8 inch layer of soil on top of the newspaper. Avoid planting mixes unless they are labeled topsoil.

·APRIL·

GROWING UP

By April, all but the coldest parts of the Rockies and high desert areas are starting to show some signs of life. You have done all your good planning and homework in January, February, and March, so you are well prepared for the whirlwind of gardening activities that need your attention this month. Weeds will be coming on strong, and edibles may need some tending.

TO DO THIS MONTH

PLAN

- If your tomato, pepper, and eggplant seedlings didn't do well, purchase some.

PREPARE AND MAINTAIN

ZONE 3

- Set out new strawberry plants, cane berries, blue berries, and rhubarb.
- Stay ahead of the bugs.
- Be sure to open the cold frame during the day so the plants don't "cook."
- Stay ahead of the weeds this month.

SOW AND PLANT

EVERYONE

- Thin out transplants to their recommended spacing intervals: beets, carrots, onions, chard, and such.
- Sow more arugula, Asian greens, cut-and-come-again lettuces.

ZONES 3 AND 4

- Plant into the garden: beets, broccoli, Brussels sprouts, cabbage, carrots, cauliflower, collards, kale, onions (green and bulb), peas, potatoes, radishes, rutabagas, shallots, spinach, turnips.
- Start seeds indoors: green onions, peppers, rutabagas, summer squash, winter squash, tomatoes.

ZONES 5 AND 6

- Transplant or direct sow into the garden: arugula, Asian greens , broccoli, Brussels sprouts, cabbages, carrots, cauliflower, chard, collards, kale, kohlrabi, lettuces, mustard greens, peas, potatoes, radishes, rutabagas, shallots, spinach and turnips.
- Plant small succession plantings of lettuce, Asian greens, spinach, and arugula.
- If the soil is warm, plant another batch of potatoes and start planting beans; repeat every two weeks.

ZONE 7

- At the end of April, in our warmest areas (Lewiston, Walla Walla, more southern parts of Utah, and Nevada), set out tomatoes, eggplants, squash, and peppers.
- Plant sunflowers at the edge of the garden.
- Sow into the garden: bush and pole beans, cantaloupes and muskmelons, cauliflower (first of the month only), corn, cucumbers, eggplants, kale, peppers, potatoes, summer squash, winter squash, watermelons.

TO DO THIS MONTH ...CONTINUED

HARVEST

- Arugula
- Asian greens
- Chives
  Fennel
- Lettuce
- Small salad greens (thinnings of beets, chard, and radishes)

You will also—hopefully—have your favorite plant protectors at hand and be prepared for any late snow flurries. New gardeners beware: several warms days in succession—maybe even a couple of warm weeks in a row—may lull you into thinking spring has sprung. But in the higher elevations, we aren't quite ready for prime time, and any town can be surprised by sudden temperature dips.

Warming Up

Use your soil thermometer to see if the soil is warm enough to plant. In most parts of the region, it should be warm enough now to harvest some tiny radish seedlings and, after thoroughly washing them, toss them whole into a salad. Some parts of the region, however, are slow to warm up. You can actually jumpstart the process of gardening by prewarming your soil. Start with a double layer of clear or red transparent plastic. Position it over the soil and hold it down with a few strategically placed bricks or stones. In a matter of days, the soil temperature can be pushed up about 10 degrees. Raised beds are likely to be warmer, too.

Greens planted and pushed along in the cold frame will be ready for fresh salads. All thinnings of beets and chard can be used this way. Tiny blossoms from organic pansies, Johnny jump-ups (violas), and violets lend an intriguing fragrance and sparkle to any salad or spring platter.

Keep up with your weeding this month. As they start to mature, weeds set seeds that you don't want to battle for years to come. Methodically remove the weeds as they appear, top dressing planting beds with compost as you go, and mulching paths after they have been cleared of weeds. The mulch will be a big help in deterring new weeds.

Pesky Little Devils

The good, the bad, and the ugly are upon us. I mean earwigs. And slugs. They love our gardens. To arrest their development, there are several tricks you can try. Set out a loosely rolled up newspaper in the garden, and leave it overnight. The following morning, quickly remove the paper and put it in a disposable bag, tied with a knot, and toss in the trash. Repeat this process the following night.

SUCCESSION PLANTING

Thomas Jefferson had a great idea for salad greens: every week he planted a thimble full of lettuce seed. Succession seeding—or planting a few more seeds of each crop at regular intervals—will extend your fresh harvest throughout the season. Bush beans, pole beans, and cut-and-come-again salad greens, and other greens are perfect choices for succession planting. Even when the weather turns hot, some greens will be ready to harvest while others are diminishing.

To deter those slimy slugs, organically, gather up your used eggshells and coffee grounds in a bucket or sturdy box. Let them dry out and mix them together, crushing the shells with your hands. Sprinkle this mixture around the base of your vegetable and fruit plants. Slugs do not like the coarse texture and will turn away.

Be vigilant for aphids, leaf miners, cutworms, and other pesky pests on your new greens and other garden plants. Wash them off or remove them at the first sign of trouble.

Herps

Gardens are not complete without a small space for herbs. Folks who don't have space for growing vegetables will want to carve out a spot—maybe just a very large flower pot or a planter box in a space that receives full sun. Herbs of all kinds have a long and storied past. Until the late 1800s, most gardeners had a sound working knowledge of herbs. In fact, some of the very first books ever produced and printed were the early "herbals"—volumes detailing the culinary, aromatic, medicinal, and magical uses of herbs.

Fresh herbs add a dimension to cooking that store-bought dried herbs can rarely match. A few sprigs of fresh parsley, basil, thyme, and tarragon added to a bowl of lettuce will elevate it to a super salad bowl. A sprig of fresh-cut mint makes the renowned mint julep. And I can't imagine Asian or Mexican food without fresh cilantro. Parsley is the basis for the Middle Eastern salad tabbouleh, and basil is the basic herb in Italian pesto.

The essential and well-known culinary herbs and their growing instructions can be found in the Edibles A to Z section of this book. Following is a sample of some of the lesser known, but wonderful edible or useful gardening herbs.

- Borage, the herb of gladness, has exquisite star-shaped blue flowers that are bee magnets. The young leaves and honey-flavored flowers can be added to salad or frozen in ice cubes to decorate a glass of lemonade.
- Chamomile, especially the Flora Pleno or Roman variety, makes a calming tea, a pleasant hair rinse particularly favored by folks with blond hair, and serves handsomely as a great pollinator host for the edible garden. It has a clean apple scent, finely feathered foliage, and Flora Pleno has double white flowers.

OUT OF GARDEN PLOT SPACE?

Try the woven, breathable fabric grow bags available at your local nursery or by mail order. Fill with potting mix and plant like a container. Another quick solution: Round up a dozen concrete blocks. Lay them out in a rectangle and fill the center area with a good soil mix. Presto!

Instant raised bed for planting. If you haven't prepared the soil underneath, don't worry. Just plant your more shallow-rooted edibles in this space: strawberries and salad greens are perfect.

- Comfrey is not grown for culinary use, but you can harvest the leaves—an excellent source of protein, nitrogen, phosphorus, and potassium—to make an organic garden tea that is a wonderful garden fertilizer. Look for a sterile variety named Bocking 14. To make the tea, fill the bottom third of a clean trashcan with comfrey cuttings. Fill the container with water and let it steep as long as six weeks. (It is smelly, so put it where it won't be noticed.) Use the tea to water all but the root crops in your garden; comfrey is so potent it can cause beets, carrots, and turnips to bolt. Wear long sleeves or gloves when handling comfrey. Leaves and stems of comfrey are covered in bristly hairs, which for some people may be a skin irritant.
- Lovage looks like parsley but tastes like celery. It can grow as tall as 4 feet!
- Winter savory, with a flavor between sage and rosemary, is a favorite in my garden. I use it with poultry dishes and pork.

Transplanting and Potting Up

This month, the process of transplanting and "potting up" should be under way. Small seedlings and plants in small germination pots need to be put into pots at least one size larger. If you think you will have to hold off on planting the transplanted vegetables and herbs a while, move each into a 1-gallon pot to allow plenty of room for their roots to develop and become strong.

If you have tomato, pepper, eggplant, or tomatillo seedlings that are ready to be moved into the next size pot, it's easy to do. Have the new pots ready to go. They should be just a size or two larger than the cell packs and clean, having been washed in warm soapy water to which a drop of bleach was added, rinsed, and dried. Fill each container halfway with a good potting mix, even a mix made of half potting mix and half good garden soil. You are aiming for a very friable, lightweight soil that will encourage strong root growth in the new plants.

Carefully remove the seedling from its cell pack or starter tray, and ever so gently, lift it, root ball and all, and place it into a hole you have prepared in the soil in the larger pot. Gently backfill around the transplant, patting down the soil a bit as you go. You don't want huge air pockets but you also don't want to compact the growing medium. Water thoroughly and gently and put back in bright light.

If you are transplanting into the garden, create a hole to accommodate the root ball of the existing seedling. Gently put this entire plant and root ball into the new space. Pat down slightly. Cover with an elevated row cover or hot caps if you anticipate unruly weather. Most lettuces and greens can withstand some cold.

In this busy month of April, as you plant, keep in mind that what you grow can be turned into delicious garden gifts. Herbs can be made into teas, sachets, and baked goods. Vegetables and fruits can be preserved and attractively packed as jams, compotes, and salsas. Take a peek at the December chapter for more ideas on gifts from the garden.

SKILL SET

MAKING ORGANIC MANURE TEA

You can make your own liquid gold or manure tea for the garden with very little effort and expense. Do not use manure tea on root crops.

You will need:

- 4 cups organic manure
- 16-inch square piece of old pillowcase, dishtowel, or cheesecloth, for making the tea bag
- String or a twist tie
- 5-gallon (or larger) plastic bucket

1 Make a tea bag by laying out the fabric on a flat surface.

2 Put 4 cups of manure in the center of the fabric, then draw the fabric up into a hobo bag packet, and secure it with the string or zip tie.

3 Put the packet in the bucket and fill the bucket with water to within a few inches of the top.

4 Let the packet steep in the bucket for 2 days.

5 Remove 2 cups of this concentrated tea to a larger container, a clean 1-gallon milk jug is good, dilute with more water to the color of weak tea, and apply 2 cups of this weak tea to each garden plant. Remove the tea bag, open it, put the manure in the compost or the garden, and discard the fabric and string or reuse.

BOUNTIFUL, BEAUTIFUL BORDERS

My grandmother occasionally admonished me to "make myself useful as well as ornamental." Is it any wonder, then, that I applied this adage to my gardens? I tuck the edibles right in with my ornamentals, and sometimes the edibles are the ornamentals. Just nestle beefsteak tomato plants between the ninebark shrubs and wait for gorgeous red fruits to play against the bronze ninebark leaves—sensational! Or for a silvery moonlight-themed garden, try planting a combination of a silvery gray-green artichoke plant, flanked by large edible sage plants, and complemented with dark purple flowering lavender, which has soft gray foliage.

TO DO THIS MONTH

PLAN

- Be alert for late freezes.

PREPARE AND MAINTAIN

- Keep up with weeding, and patrol for pests.
- Thwart wily cutworms by placing bands of copper (cutworm collars) around transplants and seedlings.
- Entice earwigs with folded up newspapers.
- Apply the coffee ground–eggshell slug deterrent.
- Remove blossoms from newly planted June-bearing strawberry plants.
- Keep the soil moist for newly seeded edibles and tender transplants.

TO DO THIS MONTH ...CONTINUED

SOW AND PLANT

ZONES 3 AND 4

- At the very end of May, in the warmest parts of your garden, if weather permits, you may be able to:
- Transplant into the garden: eggplants, tomatillos, tomatoes, peppers, squash, and other warm-weather edibles.
- Direct sow seeds for: arugula, Asian greens, bush and pole beans (and dry, snap), beets, broccoli, Brussels sprouts, cabbages, cantaloupes and muskmelons, carrots, cauliflower, chard, corn, cucumbers, kale, lettuces, mustard greens, green and bulb onions, parsnips, peas, potatoes, radishes, rutabagas, summer squash, winter squash, turnips, watermelons.
- You can still plant: asparagus, celery, kohlrabi, spinach, turnips, and rhubarb.
- Plant some Malabar climbing spinach (*Basella rubra* or *B. alba*), and provide some 6-foot posts for it to climb.

ZONES 5 AND 6

- Plant all the edibles listed for zones 3 and 4.
- Plant basil.
- Start hilling up potatoes.

ZONE 7

- Direct sow: arugula, Asian greens, basil, bush and pole beans, corn, cucumbers, eggplants, peppers, summer squash, tomatoes, watermelons, winter squash.
- Pinch back herbs, especially basil if it is getting tall.
- Continue hilling up potatoes.

HARVEST

- Arugula
- Asian greens (baby bok choy, tatsoi)
- Asparagus
- Basil
- Beans (zone 7)
- Beets, beet greens
- Brussels sprouts
- Cabbage (zone 7)
- Chard
- Garlic scapes
- Herbs
- Lettuces
- Mizuna (Japanese mustard greens)
- Pea pods and tendrils
- Radishes
- Rhubarb (from established patches)
- Rutabagas (zone 7)
- Scallions (green onions)
- Spinach
- Squash (summer) (zone 7)
- Strawberries (end of May)
- Turnips (baby, zone 7)

A royal theme would include anything gold—edible calendula flowers come to mind—with the aubergine of dark purple eggplants. Think vertical and imagine how stately, yet productive, a tower of purple pole beans will be, standing in the rose bed?

Our Fickle May

While the warmest parts of the intermountain west can experience surprisingly warm temperatures in May, it is not uncommon to have late-season snowstorms, maybe even into June. Be ready with row covers, hot caps, and Wall o' Water season extenders to protect the most tender plants and transplants. If your garden is in the path of frequent winds, especially Washoe Zephyrs and blasts from the Arctic Express, you may want to construct a simple windbreak out of stakes and horticulture fabric to shield groups of tender plants or individual plants.

Birds seem to have an affinity for newly sprouted seedlings, and rabbits love lettuce. And your garden will

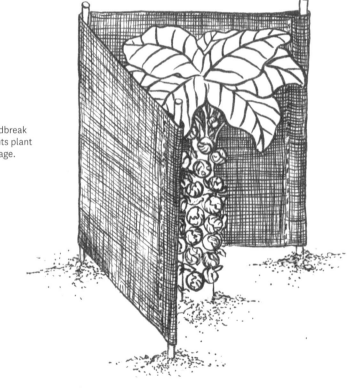

This simple two-sided windbreak around this Brussels sprouts plant protects it from wind damage.

disappear if you haven't fended off the deer. Make sure your garden plots are protected from the eager feeders.

Watch for the first spears of asparagus, around the first of the month. If we have a nice rain followed by a warm spell, the asparagus will shoot up out of the ground. In the past, the practice was to forgo the first two seasons' harvest, allowing the plant to build up strength. New and improved varieties don't need to be babied, but it is still wise to take only a few spears the first season, a few more the second. Snap the spears off at the soil line when they are the size you want. Alternately, you can use a sharp paring knife and cut them cleanly about 1 inch above the soil.

Also in May, hardneck garlic varieties will send out some wild-looking, curling tendrils at the top of the plant's main stalk. This is called a garlic scape, and is considered by many to be a spring delicacy. It is nothing more than the flower stalk of the garlic plant, and the bent part of the stem, above the node where it connects, will develop small garlic bulbils (small, new baby bulbs of the parent plant) if left to grow. It is best to remove the scape (it snaps off easily where it connects to the stem) and enjoy eating it, and let the plant put its energy into developing full garlic bulbs underground.

Heirloom gardeners often re-create the historical Native American Three Sisters Garden. Children and adults alike are captivated by this type of planting. The "three sisters" are corn, beans, and squash, and are planted in a group on a mound. Sunflowers are usually planted nearby. Plant tall corn in the center, with pole beans at the base of the corn (when it comes up). The beans will twine up the corn. Squash is planted in between and allowed to ramble, and so it shades the soil. The beans have the added advantage of being nitrogen fixers, offsetting the heavy-feeder corn and squash plants. There is some speculation that the squash is also a deterrent to raccoons, since the squash vines are prickly and inhospitable to the critters. Nutritionally, this vegetable trio makes a perfect protein food combination very rich in fiber.

Start a Support Group for Your Garden

Have all the stakes, cages, supports, nets, and trellises in position as soon as possible—the sooner the better, to avoid damaging a plant's root system. You can build your own trellises or repurpose other materials as the support. You may not realize it but you probably have a treasure trove of plant supports lollygagging around in your garage. Old chains, multi-paned window frames without glass, pieces of fencing—all of these are easily adapted as supports for climbing beans, cucumbers, and trombone-style climbing zucchini. Bicycle tires fastened to fences or poles make swirling, intriguing supports for vining plants.

TIP *Zucchetta Tromboncino zucchini is an interesting heirloom squash that invites conversation. It is a climber that reaches 8 to 10 feet. Once it's up and going, let it spread out: it's great for screening out an annoying neighbor. These squash resemble trombones; they are delicious when cooked and have very few seeds. For eating, harvest when they are still young and only 12 to 18 inches long.*

Tomato Wars

There is great debate among gardeners about whether to stake or cage tomatoes. Having used both systems, I prefer staking. First, it allows for maximum air circulation in and around the plant and the resulting fruits. Second, it's easier to locate a chomping hornworm in a tall, staked plant than in a densely packed caged tomato. And the open, staked method makes it much easier to locate the ripe tomatoes ready for harvest. Stakes should be very sturdy, capable of supporting 25 to 30 pounds of weight. Use flexible ties that won't cut into the expanding, growing stem or trunk of the plant. A strip of pantyhose makes a terrific soft tie. Position the stake the same time you place the tiny tomato plant in the ground. Keep the stake within 3 to 6 inches of the plant, and sink it into the soil at least 12 inches deep. Use a rubber mallet to pound it down securely. As the tomato grows, tie the main stem gently to the stake, and check the ties often to make sure they are not strangling the stem.

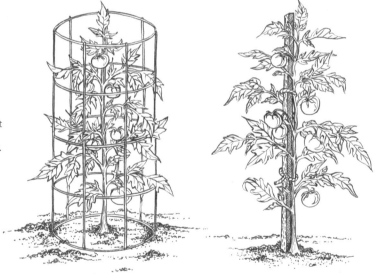

For improved air circulation and accessibility, securely staking a tomato plant to a single, sturdy post is recommended. Some gardeners prefer to "cage" their tomato plants. Either method will work.

In our arid climate, you will give tomato seedlings a growing advantage by planting them as deep as their first set of leaves. Remove the leaves before back-filling the planting hole with soil, and the main stem will sprout new roots.

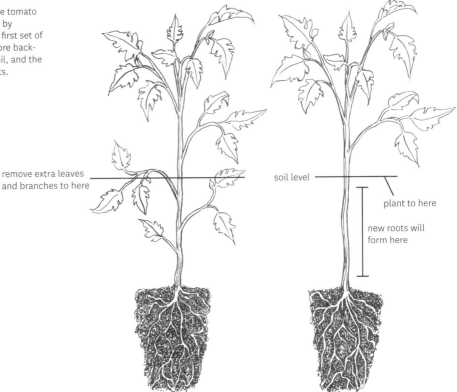

remove extra leaves
and branches to here

soil level

plant to here

new roots will
form here

With peppers and eggplants, cages seem to be a better choice. They keep the plant corralled so the leaves provide some shade for the easily blistered fruits. Cages can be constructed of metal or wood. Position the cages at the same time you set out the small transplants of eggplants and peppers. Make sure the cages are securely placed in the soil, by using a rubber mallet to tap it into place.

Here is a planting trick for encouraging strong tomato plants. Tomato plants are all about their root development: the bigger and better the root system, the bigger and better the plant. To give them a little extra rooting capability, plant each tomato plant deep enough to cover the first set of leaves off the main stem, but remove those leaves that would be buried before you plant. Those buried leafless stems will send out roots and strengthen the entire plant.

This brings us to another tomato controversy. Do you or don't you remove the suckers (the branches that sprout out at the junction of the main stem and the side branches)? Some gardeners pinch them off, with the theory that they sap the energy of the plant, which should go to the main branches bearing the ripening tomatoes. You can experiment with this idea throughout your tomato patch, and see what you think the answer is. As soon as your tomato seedlings start to grow, keep a watchful eye for the little suckers. If you are growing indeterminate varieties of tomatoes, or tomatoes that grow upward and bear over a long period of time, pruning away the suckers may keep the plant from becoming top heavy and splitting as it matures. Nip these out as soon as you see them. Determinate plants do not require sucker pruning since they are more compact, bushy tomato plants and produce fruit pretty much all at once.

Waste No Space

Hot sunny spaces never go to waste in the thoughtfully planned edible garden. Feathery fennel and dill make thrilling additions in the ornamental garden or in container plantings and act as host plants for sought-after pollinators. They add airy, ferny texture to the garden. Include heat-loving, drought-tolerant nasturtiums, thyme, oregano, and calendulas to spill over the edges of sun-loving containers. Grown organically, the colorful flower petals of these choices are a surprising, tasty addition to salads. Tuck all these plants in among shrubs and vegetables for added garden interest, good eating, and potentially increased yield.

SKILL SET

HILLING YOUR SPUDS

Potatoes do very well grown in a hill. Since potatoes produce tubers along the length of their root system, it's advantageous to grow them in hills or raised mounds. In the garden, dig either a series of 12-inch-wide holes 6 inches deep or a 12-inch-wide furrow 6 inches deep. Stack the soil from the holes up on the side. Drop the chitted potato into the hole or, if using the long furrow, space the seed potatoes at the bottom 12 to 16 inches apart. Cover the potato(s) with a couple of inches of soil. When the green leaves emerge, push more of the leftover soil up around the plant but keep the leaves exposed to catch some sun. Repeat a few times until you have run out of extra soil and you have created a potato mound or long, raised, tunnel-type of row. The potatoes will develop happily in their dark underground space.

LOOKING GOOD IN GREEN

Now is the time to pull it all together. In all but the highest elevations, it's warm enough to have everything planted and ready to grow. In Elko, Butte, Baker, or Burns, you may still have to protect the "hotties"—tomatoes, eggplants, and cucumbers—plants that love and need warm weather and lots of sun. In the rest of the Rocky Mountain region, your garden should be planted, weeded, hoses ready, growing supports in place, paths mulched, pest deterrents set out, and a big jug of manure tea brewed and ready to go. Treat yourself and your family to some of the garden jewels at hand now: strawberries, rhubarb, and bright green sugar snap peas galore.

TO DO THIS MONTH

PLAN

- Make note of the last frost date that occurred in your garden.
- Purchase extra seed packets for cut-and-come-again lettuces and greens.
- Clean your canning and freezing gear so it's ready to use.

PREPARE AND MAINTAIN

- Mulch some more.
- Watch your newly sprouting salad greens for munching insects and birds.
- If you are setting out transplants, put out cutworm collars.
- Keep the compost pile cooking by adding to it and tossing regularly.
- Drench the soil around all but the root crop plants with diluted manure tea.
- Check the sprinkler and irrigation systems to make sure they are in top working order.

TO DO THIS MONTH ... CONTINUED

SOW AND PLANT

EVERYONE

- You can still make weekly plantings of bush and pole beans.
- Plant some more sunflower seeds.
- Plant another row of basil between the tomato plants.

ZONES 3 AND 4

- Transplant or direct sow: basil, beets, broccoli, Brussels sprouts, carrots, cauliflower, chard, corn, kale, lettuces, mustard greens, radishes, and turnips.
- At first of the month, plant short-season: cantaloupes and muskmelons, cucumbers, watermelons, peppers, tomatoes, potatoes, and summer and winter squash.

ZONES 5 AND 6

- Plant first week of month: corn, cucumbers, eggplants, peppers, tomatoes, summer and winter squash, watermelons.

ZONE 7

- It's getting too hot to plant anything other than the most tolerant small greens.

HARVEST

- Arugula
- Asian greens
- Beans (zone 7)
- Beet greens
- Broccoli (zone 7)
- Brussels sprouts (zone 7)
- Cabbages (zone 7)
- Chard
- Garlic scapes
- Herbs
- Kale
- Lettuces
- Mustard greens
- Nasturtium flowers and violets
- Onions (both green and bulb)
- Peas and pea tendrils
- Peppers (zone 7)
- Potatoes (zones 5 to 7)
- Radishes
- Raspberries
- Rhubarb
- Rutabagas
- Spinach
- Strawberries
- Tomatoes (zone 7)

Mother Nature is Full of Surprises

You never know what Mother Nature is going to do. But by keeping a garden journal—or simply noting important weather events on a calendar—you will have a record of what worked last year and *could* happen from year to year. As our weather patterns become more unusual, it pays to be prepared.

Was the spring last year so wet you had to plant peas, beans, or corn a second time? Basil three times? If you have an automated irrigation system with timed sprinklers, when did you first turn it on for the season? What date were you able to set out the tomatoes based on the soil temperatures? Make a note of the final night you had to cover your tomatoes and other frost-tender plants for the season. If you made a 30-gallon container of manure tea, how long did it last? Record the dates when you sowed the seeds directly in the garden, and the germination dates of the seeds you so carefully tended.

Tending the Garden

Generally we are so excited about fresh strawberries and peas, we stare at them, willing them to ripen before our watchful eyes. Once you start to enjoy the fruits of your labor, it's just as important to stay on top of the daily pickings in order keep the plant producing as long as possible. Cover plants with netting to keep the birds from beating you to the harvest.

Here's a little mnemonic device for June gardens: the three Ms—mulch, moisture, and manicure. If someone you know has an organically tended lawn, use the grass clippings to line the pathways in the vegetable garden. As the mulch packs down, add a new layer. Yes, mulch, mulch, and mulch some more if you haven't already created a nice cooling, weed-thwarting barrier throughout your garden. As the days heat up, mulch keeps the roots of the plants protected and cool. Mulch helps the soil hold moisture, slowing evaporation on warm days. Should weeds decide to poke through, it is easy to see them and pluck them right out. Mulch is indeed a fabulous thing. I like to add a nice top dressing of organic compost to my largest containers now, too.

Most plants like a little boost now and then. Be lavish with that manure tea concoction. Spread it around, generously dousing the roots of thirsty hotties on a regular basis. It's a good idea to make a note of these applications on the calendar or in the journal.

The need for consistent and regular garden watering will pick up now. Unless you are on a flood irrigation program, water costs a pretty penny. After watering thoroughly, stick your finger down into the soil, a few inches from a plant. The soil should be damp at least 6 inches down. Check emitters to be sure they are clear of debris and flowing freely. If using sprinkler spray heads, observe them in action and see if they arc, in fact, spraying the plants you want them to get to. Double-check pop-up heads and hoses on timers for efficacy and reliability. Don't even think of going on vacation without asking someone to oversee the watering of your vegetable garden.

Support Those Vines

As the cucumbers, melons, and squash develop beyond their first sets of leaves, be ready to train them up supports, if that is your method of growing them this season. Cucumbers and melons do exceptionally well on screen-type or sheep-fencing support systems. Made of galvanized wire, generally sold in panels measuring 4 by 8 feet, with 4-inch squares, this type of fencing is strong, durable, and reusable. Lean the fencing against two support posts at about a 70-degree angle. It is capable of holding up cantaloupes and other small melons. If using it straight up, secure it firmly upright between two posts. Old strips of mesh, panty hose, or cheesecloth can be used as slings to hold the melons. Let cucumbers hang down to keep them long and straight (see illustration, page 44).

TIP *After harvesting delicate berries, gently but thoroughly rinse them in a sink of cool, clear water to wash off any dust or bugs. Put them in a solution of 3 cups of water with 1 cup of white vinegar. Drain carefully in a colander or dry on paper or cloth towels. Store in a paper towel–lined container in the refrigerator. The vinegar will slow the growth of bacteria and mildew and prolong the keeping time of the berries.*

SKILL SET

MAKING HERB CUBES

Harvest and rinse any single herb or a combination of herbs. Coarsely chop them and put 1 tablespoon of herbs in each cell of a plastic ice cube tray. Top off each cell with a generous glug of olive oil. Freeze. When frozen solid, remove the herb cubes from the tray and seal them in a strong freezer bag. In the cold, dark days of winter, you will love adding these to a pot of pasta sauce or a cruet of salad dressing.

·JULY·

SOME LIKE IT HOT

In a perfect world, our Julys would be about 85°F during the daytime and a cool 50°F at night for nurturing vegetables in the garden. So often, though, in the warmer parts of our region, day-time temps shoot up and over the 100°F mark and the evenings don't get cool enough. But now is when all your good garden preparation will pay off. All that mulch you laid out is keep-ing the roots of your plants cool and happy. The carefully organized watering system is putting moisture down where it needs to be, at the roots of the plants, and those pesky weeds get none! Eggplants and tomatoes are starting to set fruits, and new potatoes can be dug. Fresh green beans are ready to be picked. Raspberries? Yum!

TO DO THIS MONTH

PLAN

- After you've finished a second sowing, make note of the seeds you've used up.
- Organize your seed collection in order and put it away in a dark, dry, cool place.
- Count your canning jar lids and rings and freezer containers. Be ready for abundant harvests.

PREPARE AND MAINTAIN

- Keep a watchful eye on squash and melon plants for squash bugs.
- Strawberry "daughters" can be encouraged to root now.
- Keep tomatoes staked up, gently securing them as they reach for the sun.
- Remove spent pea vines from the garden and add them to the compost heap.
- Keep the compost pile cooking by adding to it and tossing it regularly.
- Time for another application of comfrey or manure tea—for all the hotties, especially.
- Check the sprinklers again. Timers should be updated and all the spray nozzles checked for spray patterns.
- Keep vegetables, fruits, berries, and herbs picked to encourage production.

SOW AND PLANT

EVERYONE

- You can still make weekly plantings of bush beans.
- Time for the second planting of arugula, basil, beets, chard, kale, Asian greens, carrots, Malabar spinach.
- In the coolest part of the garden, sow a bit more lettuce.
- Check the mint plants. A large container dedicated solely to unruly mint is a great idea.

ZONES 3 AND 4

- Seed or transplant out broccoli, Brussels sprouts, green onions, lettuces, radishes, scallions, spinach.

TO DO THIS MONTH ...CONTINUED

HARVEST

- Arugula
- Asian greens
- Beans
- Beets
- Blackberries
- Broccoli
- Cabbages
- Cantaloupes and muskmelons (zone 7)
- Carrots
- Cauliflower (zones 5 and 6)
- Chard
- Collards (all but hottest areas)
- Corn (zones 6 and 7)
- Cucumbers
- Eggplant
- Garlic
- Herbs
- Kale (zones 3 to 6)
- Lettuces (unlikely in zone 7 with high heat)
- Onions (scallions and bulbs)
- Parsnips (zone 7)
- Potatoes
- Radishes
- Raspberries
- Rutabagas (zone 7)
- Spinach
- Squash blossoms
- Squash (summer) (zones 5 to 7)
- Tomatoes (zones 5 to 7)
- Turnips (zone 7)
- Watermelon (zone 7)

By planting small, tender plants under tall, bushy ones, you give the newbies a chance to set down roots and grow strong before subjecting them to the daily rigors of our western sunshine and heat.

More Planting

Late July is the time to plant a second round of some edibles, particularly chard, arugula, cutting lettuces, beets, carrots, another hill of bush beans, and even a bit more basil if you think you will need it. This will extend your fresh harvest into autumn. It's so warm now, all of these seeds will sprout up in half the time they did in the spring. And when the mercury climbs, you'll be glad you planted that Malabar spinach in May. The young leaves are good torn into salads while the older ones are great cooked.

Underplanting, succession planting, intercropping, and companion planting are good tricks to have up your gardener's sleeve:

- Underplanting means to fill the area under and around a larger, taller plant with smaller new plants.
- Succession planting is the method of following one crop with another, maximizing the yield from the garden. You can replant small amounts of a certain lettuce, for example, every ten days or so, or you can plant different lettuce varieties that mature at different times.

- Intercrop planting is mixing two or more crops together to get the most out your garden space. Tomatoes are often intercropped with basil. The basil plants appreciate a little afternoon shade from the tall, bushy tomatoes. Besides, they taste marvelous together.
- Companion planting, or putting certain plants near others for mutual benefit, has been practiced for centuries. It is often done to take advantage of the insect repelling properties of certain plants.

Underplanting a row of basil between the tomatoes keeps the hottest sun off the new basil plants, but allows enough light in for the basil to germinate and take off. Companion planting is another great way to make excellent use of any and all valuable garden real estate. Borage planted next to strawberries is said to make them sweeter and, at a minimum, attracts bees and wasps for pollination. Nasturtiums planted around the perimeter of a squash patch will attract aphids, and hopefully

By planting different crops together, you give them certain advantages, such as basil under tomatoes getting shade, and lettuce under beans gaining coolness.

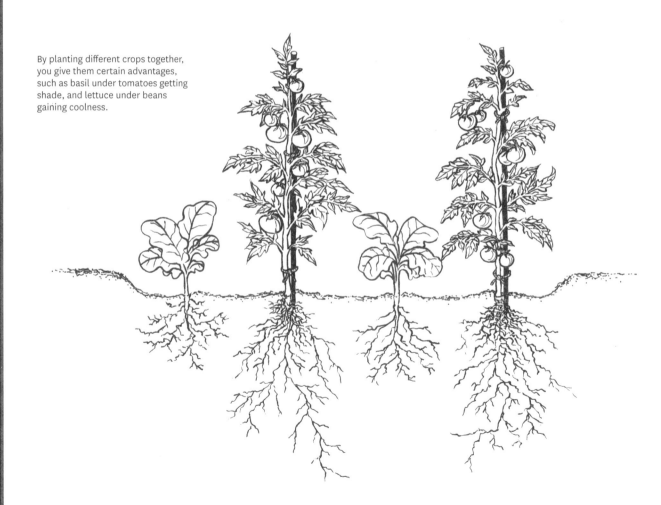

squash borers, keeping them from the valuable squash plants. Intercropping is a method of planting cool-season crops for fall while it's still hot. You can plant peas, spinach, broccoli, cauliflower, Asian greens, arugula, chard, and lettuces in July and August for harvest in September and October. In milder areas, harvesting can extend into winter.

When seeding in late summer, plant your seeds a little deeper than you would in the spring, to take advantage of cooler soil and moisture. Shading the newly planted seeds and seedlings will help protect them from the hot summer sun. Mulch, row covers, and taller plants, such as your mature tomatoes, can be used for this.

Picking and Tending

It seems like a no-brainer to keep vegetables, fruits, berries, and herbs picked. But often, we get caught up in summer fun, and become overwhelmed by the abundance of the garden or the heat, and we let another day go by without checking the zucchini plants, cucumbers, beans, and herbs. They thrive by being picked! So stay on top of harvesting the bounty. It also keeps the plants—and the garden as a whole—tidy.

Regular inspection of the vines and stalks and stems will keep you alert to unwanted pests. I've often discovered the ugly tomato hornworm when I was just inspecting the plants. It is good to keep the herbs in check as well: A fresh haircut for the thyme, tarragon, and sage will cause a fresh flush of new leaves for cooking and keeps the plant shapely and from going to seed.

If aphids and spider mites are present, put a good spray nozzle on your garden hose and give the garden and any fruit trees a strong, cold, shower. And, as ghastly as it sounds, pick and trash hornworms and squash bugs if you come across them in the garden.

Strawberry daughters are the baby plants that grow at the end of the main plant's "runners." To make them take root, use a branched twig or a clothespin to gently peg them against the soil where you want them to grow.

To pick blackberries, look for those that are deep black with a plump, full feeling. A ripe berry will pull free from the plant with only a slight tug. If the berry is red or purple, it's not ripe yet.

County Fair Contests

If you are of a competitive spirit, consider entering the vegetables or fruits of your garden labor in your local fair. Each year, communities around the county hold fun-filled county fairs. You'll get to see what other folks have grown, and you can even put your garden skills on the line. Enter your best cucumber, tomato, Walla Walla onion, or fill-in-the-blank vegetable or fruit or both for the largest, prettiest, or tastiest in dozens of categories. Start preening now. Shelter that special tomato from all danger, be it weather or critter related. Maybe another good drink of comfrey or manure tea is in order? Entries are judged on several criteria: general appearance, uniformity, and conformity. Appearance means clean and of edible quality, picked at the time of appropriate ripeness with no obvious bruising or blemishes, insect and disease free; uniformity means all specimens must be of the same size, shape and color; and conformity to specifications of class means the edible was entered in the correct class, with the exact number of specimens and the variety name clearly indicated. Start grooming your candidates now, pick up an exhibitor booklet of rules, and get ready to be a part of this wonderful tradition.

SKILL SET

SOME JULY ACTIVITIES

Here's some fun things to do this month:

Harvest squash blossoms. In July, the number of zucchini and yellow crookneck squash may already be getting the best of you. There's an easy, elegant, and delicious way to deal with them: nip them in the bud. Yes, go right ahead and gently remove some of the blossoms. It's a good idea to harvest them in the morning when they have just fully opened. Be sure you haven't captured any tag-along passengers, especially bees! Gently but thoroughly rinse the flowers, and pat them dry with paper towels. Remove the stamens and any visible seeds. Stuff with rice or soft cheese and herbs, then sauté or deep-fry. If they are female blossoms, they may have tiny squash attached at the base. Leave them connected to the blossom.

Harvest and store garlic (end of July/early August in most areas). Just a few months ago, you plugged little cloves of garlic (pointed end up) into the garden and waited patiently. Now it's time to get them out of the ground and ready for the pantry. Knowing the perfect time to harvest garlic is a bit tricky. Carefully brush back the soil and look carefully at the bulbs: Do they have solid looking shoulders and are they filled out nicely? Sometimes you just have to go in with a trowel and have a peek. Gently and carefully dig straight down beside the formed garlic bulb, loosening it from the soil, and lifting it upward. Using your hands, carefully remove the bulb from the soil and inspect it for fullness and size. (Don't try to just pull the bulb out of the ground.) Brush off the soil, and remove the garlic to a cool, dry place to cure. If the bulbs are not quite filled out and ready, leave them another week or so. If they are ready, then harvest, cure, and store. To cure garlic in preparation for storage, hang the bare bulbs with their foliage in bundles or spread them out on a table or rack. You can eat them right away, but garlic bulbs intended for storage must be cured first so they don't rot.

Make mint tea. Bring a large pot of clean water almost to a boil, then turn off the heat. Add four or five black tea bags and a huge handful of freshly cut and washed mint sprigs to the pot. Cover and let rest for 10 minutes. Cool and enjoy over ice.

·AUGUST·

BRING IT ON

August is the month of second chances in the garden. Okay, maybe it's your third or fourth round of planting for the year, but August is a great time to plant. Those hot August days and nights make the soil warm and perfect for starting a new crop of leafy green vegetables. The seeds have a chance to germinate quickly and get off to a strong start before the arrival of crisp fall days. Corn by the bushel is ready for shucking. Take a deep breath. The harvest is here.

TO DO THIS MONTH

PLAN

ZONES 3 AND 4

- Put your seed collection in order and then tuck it away in a dark, dry, cool, secure spot.

ZONES 5 TO 7

- At the beginning of the month, make a date with the garden for sowing fall vegetables.
- Keep track of your harvests (by amount, weight) in your garden journal or calendar.

PREPARE AND MAINTAIN

- Keep up with a regular, deep, thorough watering regimen, and be ready to hold back the water on some areas such as potatoes, garlic, and onion plantings.
- Strawberry beds can be renovated now.
- Leave asparagus fronds in place for a while longer. Keep those beds weeded.
- Keep up with the harvest of all the produce.
- Add organic lawn clippings to the compost pile, and give the pile a couple of good turns.
- Remove plants that have given their all. Compost them, if they are disease free.

TO DO THIS MONTH ...CONTINUED

SOW AND PLANT

ZONES 3 AND 4

- Sow arugula, Asian greens, beets, beets, lettuce, spinach, turnips.
- Check end-of-season sales for cane fruits. Both can be planted now for harvests next year.

ZONES 5 AND 6

- After the hottest part of the month, you can set out new plants of the hardiest herbs: savory, oregano, tarragon, parsley.
- There is still time to grow another fresh crop of basil for making late-season pesto.
- Mid-late month: Plant arugula, Asian greens, beans, lettuces.

ZONE 7

- Sow arugula, Asian greens, basil, beans, beets, carrots, collards, lettuces, mustard greens, early maturing summer squash, and turnips.

HARVEST

- Arugula
- Asian greens
- Basil
- Beans
- Beets
  (zones 3 and 4)
- Blackberries
- Blueberries
- Cabbage
- Cantaloupes and
  muskmelons
- Carrots
- Cauliflower
  (zone 3 and 4)

- Chard
- Corn
- Cucumbers
- Dill and fennel
  (fronds and
  seeds)
- Eggplant
- Garlic
- Herbs
- Onions and
  scallions
- Parsnips
  (zones 3 to 6)
- Peppers

- Potatoes
- Raspberries
  (late and
  ever-bearing,
  red and gold)
- Rutabagas
- Shallots
- Squash
  (summer)
- Squash (winter)
  (zone 7)
- Strawberries
- Tomatoes
- Watermelons

When It All Comes Together

It may seem like it took forever to get to August, but all of a sudden the garden comes together in a very big way. A month ago you were staring at the tomatoes, willing them to ripen, and now you are in tomato heaven. It is absolutely critical to keep up with the picking of cucumbers, squash, tomatoes, peppers, broccoli, Brussels sprouts, and other crops. By removing the mature fruit, you are telling the plant it needs to keep producing. More, more, and more.

As a young girl, I spent many summers in my grandmother's kitchen, where I learned that making the most of August harvests meant eating well all winter long. In those days, it was standard operating procedure to grow, can, freeze, and otherwise "put up" lots of foodstuffs for the winter table. There were no supermarkets close to the wheat farms in our rural area. We had a root cellar and it smelled of goodness: hard, damp soil and sweet carrots. August meant making good things for the pantry and cupboards.

Whether you can, freeze, or dry the produce from your garden or a farmers' market, it's wonderful just knowing your food came from the freshest beginnings, was handled with care and loving hands, and not bathed in chemicals. Everything in your garden can be harvested at the peak of perfection, and gently preserved for eating later on. Here are a couple of quick ways to harness the summer perfection of your garden.

Clean up the existing herb plants, keeping them in check, and don't let them flower. At the very least, cut off the flowers before the plants start to set seeds. Consider making pestos and herb cubes for winter use.

Pesto, the traditional condiment from Italy, has cousins and relatives in several countries. The familiar Italian-style pesto Genovese is made with fresh basil, olive oil, pine nuts, garlic, and pecorino or parmesan cheese. But when herbs are at their peak in the garden, let your culinary aspirations run free and use any combination of herbs, oils, nuts, and garlic you like. Consider pestos with a base of cilantro, oregano, or parsley. Add nuts of any kind: almonds, hazelnuts, walnuts, pecans. Maybe add some lemon or orange peel, dried red pepper, or black pepper. While pesto was originally made using a mortar and pestle, you can whip up a batch using a food processor or a blender. Add enough oil to make a thick paste, put into silicone or quick-release ice cube trays, freeze solid, then pop out the cubes and repack them in strong freezer bags or containers. Use them as needed for an easy batch of hot pasta. Make enough to share with friends.

Corn is another one of those produce items that lends itself to a quick freeze. Get a friend to help you shuck and clean a bushel or burlap bag of corn. Have big pots of water boiling on the stove. Do not salt the water; it only makes the tender kernels tough. Put some dishtowels on the counter and have another big bowl of ice water ready. Drop the cleaned ears of corn in the boiling water for 4 minutes; remove to the ice bath for 1 minute, then to the towels to dry. With a sharp knife, cutting straight down the cob, remove the kernels. Pop them by measured cupful into plastic freezer bags or containers. Carefully note the date, amount, and contents on the package. Freeze. Enjoy long after Old Man Winter arrives on your doorstep.

It is a good practice to renovate your strawberry beds from year to year. This is much easier than it sounds and is simply a means of establishing the daughter plants to replace the spent mother plants at about three years to maximize berry production in the garden. Strawberries still need plenty of moisture. Newly planted "daughters" should be developing strong root systems. Some raspberries will be setting a new crop of fruit now. Keep picking them.

Dry Storage for Root Crops and Winter Vegetables

Root crops, including potatoes, carrots, beets, turnips, rutabagas, winter radishes, kohlrabi, and parsnips, do very well in cool storage. They should be stored in an environment that is near, but not at, freezing and has a relative high humidity. Store them in bins surrounded by slightly damp sand and/or vermiculite (available at any local nursery or garden center).

Onions should be dry enough so that their skins rustle before being put into storage. They need to be in a very cold (but not freezing), low-humidity environment.

Cabbage can be stored in a cool spot, but keep it away from other vegetables because it emits ethylene gas, which can be cause premature rot in some other vegetables. Pack cabbage upside down to keep soil or debris from settling among the leaves.

Pumpkins and winter squash store well and for a long time when kept at 50 to 60°F with low humidity.

HARVESTING POTATOES AND ONIONS

Hot, dry weather is the perfect time for harvesting potatoes and onions. A trenching shovel is a favorite tool of mine, simply because the blade is long, goes deep, and works well in small spaces. Hands with gloves are the next best tool.

For potatoes, approximately ten to twelve weeks after planting, when the plants turn yellow and start to falter, carefully dig straight down, about 6 inches deep and lift the soil upward. When you see the potatoes, gently work your way around the plant, lifting the soil, and removing all the potatoes. Do not wash them, but brush the dirt off them and place them in a very cool, but not freezing, dark storage place, ideally about 40 to 50°F. Bushel baskets and open cardboard boxes make great storage bins for potatoes.

For onions, when the green stems start to deteriorate and fall over, they are almost ready for harvest. Stop watering them at this point. Since onions are nearer the surface than potatoes, use a small, long-handled shovel to gently lift the onion bulbs from the soil. If you aren't expecting rain, let them rest on the surface of the garden for a couple of days or up to a couple of weeks. They can also be moved to a dry, shady spot. When the onion necks have dried and the skins make a crispy rustling sound, the onions can be moved to a well-ventilated, cool, dry, secure storage area. Good air circulation is a must to prevent spoilage. Cut off the stems, leaving about 1 inch at the top of the onion.

GOOD AND PLENTY

September is all about abundance in the garden. In the high country, you may have had a first frost, even a dusting of snow. But throughout most of the mountain region we continue to enjoy clear days, cool evenings, and a delicious, bountiful harvest of vegetables and fruits from our very own gardens. If you like canning and preserving, there's still a bit of time to gather up apples, peaches, and enough cucumbers for pickling. Personally, I love September. The sun loses some of its summer strength, and as it sits lower in the sky, the sunsets are breathtaking. Everything about the garden slows just a bit—enough to catch our breath after the scramble of high summer.

TO DO THIS MONTH

PLAN

- Sketch out the garden as it was this year, showing what you planted and where.
- Make a note of any new and different vegetable or fruit you admired in a friend's garden or at the fair.
- Keep track of your harvests in your garden journal or calendar.
- Save your seeds.

PREPARE AND MAINTAIN

- Cover sunflower heads with mesh to keep pests off.
- Cut back on water to most of the garden. Adjust timers as needed.
- Mow down the asparagus fronds, and mulch the area.
- Keep up the harvest of produce.
- Keep adding organic lawn clippings to the compost pile. Keep the pile turned.
- Clean up the expired plants as you go. Compost plants if disease free.

SOW AND PLANT

ZONES 3 AND 4

- Plant some Asian greens and arugula in the cold frame.

ZONES 5 AND 6

- Plant Asian greens, arugula, beets, and kale.

ZONE 7

- Plant salad greens: mâche, chard, kale, arugula, lettuces, Asian greens, spinach, cabbage, and green onions.
- Plant beets, broccoli, carrots, collards, mustard greens, radishes, and turnips.
- Check Labor Day sales for cane fruits; plant now for harvest next year.

HARVEST

- Arugula
- Asian greens
- Beans
- Blackberries
- Cabbage
- Cantaloupe and muskmelons
- Carrots
- Corn
- Cucumbers
- Eggplant
- Garlic
- Herbs
- Kale
- Kohlrabi
- Onions
- Parsnips
- Peppers (sweet, hot)
- Potatoes
- Pumpkins
- Raspberries (late and ever-bearing, red and gold)
- Rutabagas
- Shallots
- Squash (summer and winter)
- Tomatoes
- Turnips

The Fall-Back Position

If August is frenzied when all finally comes to fruition, in September it seems as if everything ripens at once. There is a flurry of activity as we try to gather all the bits of goodness together, eating them up as they come out of the garden and putting up what we can for winter. Since there is not a worthy way to preserve melon, the last bites of watermelon and cantaloupe are savored. But there are many ways to hang onto the summer garden, and that's what we do in our "fall-back position."

The last of the red and green—yes, green—tomatoes: We all try to outfox Mother Nature when we start gardening. Protecting our tomatoes is something we do in April, May, and June, and again at the end of the garden year. Yes, you can throw blankets, towels, and sheets over the plants to protect them from the first couple of frosts. But that gets old quick, and a killing frost will come, turning the vines black and mushy and ruining the fruit.

It's now time to carefully place mesh onion bags or netting over the heads of the tall sunflowers to keep the birds and squirrels from stripping the flowers of their seeds. This may require a stepladder for getting to the top of these giants, so be careful. Or, if you prefer, leave the seeds for the critters.

Give the herbs one last haircut for the season. Oregano and thyme, if planted against a warm rock or wall, can often be clipped and harvested well into December. If you are bringing in the tender herbs, rosemary, and lavender, and if they are in portable growing containers, now is the time to move them next to the house, onto the porch, or into the garage. Hose them down thoroughly before bringing them indoors and inspect them for the occasional joy-riding slug or spider. Rosemary and lavender do best with a fine layer of gravel mulch on top of the soil. They need very strong bright light, so put them in a south-, southwest-, or western-facing window. Water sparingly.

As time allows, freeze, can, dry, or preserve as much of your produce as possible. If you don't have fruit trees, check out the farmers' market, the roadside fruit stands, and your local growers through the website, www.localharvest.org. Many cities and towns also participate in a kind of off-market produce market. Idaho has a terrific one, Idaho's Bounty. For a small membership fee, you can have access to locally grown meats, produce, jams, jellies, herbal products, and much more. You order via their online website once a week or every two weeks and your order is delivered to a central drop-off. My young plum trees aren't very productive yet, so I will purchase a half-bushel of Italian prune plums from that source for making plum chutney for this winter.

And don't forget to make copious notes of your garden's successes and failures. By keeping track of your garden's productivity this year, you will be better able to assess your ability and garden space for growing edibles. Did you have way too much zucchini? Maybe two plants would be enough. Are you wishing you had planted six Roma tomato plants for making Nonna's Italian tomato sauce? There is nothing more enlightening than a just-finished garden season.

Seed Saving

Why should we care about seeds? Early on in this book I called seeds—the edible computer chips—a miracle. That miracle is in jeopardy. At one time, there were hundreds of small seed companies in this county, and before that, gardeners saved their own seeds. It was what they could afford, what they knew, and what they grew. In the past few years, our seed supply has been gathered up by a handful of corporate entities and the incredible diversity and purity of our genetic lines are being compromised. If you enjoy growing your food from seed, imagine how rewarding it would be to save your own seed from year to year (gaining a certain bit of self-sufficiency) and to swap some of that special seed with like-minded fellow gardeners.

There are many terms used with regard to seed saving. Here are the most important:

- Open pollination is pollination by natural mechanisms: birds, insects, or wind.
- F1 Hybrids are the first generation made from crossing two different parent varieties, the offspring of which produce a new, uniform seed variety with specific characteristics from both parents.
- GMO seeds are from genetically modified organisms—plants or animals created through the gene splicing techniques of biotechnology (also called genetic engineering, or GE). Non-GMO seeds means the genetics have not been manipulated.
- Treated seeds are those that have been given an application of a pesticide or subjected to a process (generally a chemical process) designed to reduce, control, or repel disease organisms, insects, or other pests that attack seed or seedlings grown from seed.

- Self-pollinated plants include lettuce, spinach, peas, snap peas, lima beans and green beans, including bush and climbing varieties. Peppers such as chiles, habaneros, jalapeños, and sweet and bell peppers will also self-pollinate.
- Heirloom seed varieties generally means those that are nonindustrial, saved by hand, and were grown before WWII. They are open-pollinated and nonhybrid.
- Certified naturally grown seeds are from small organic farms. These farms do not use any synthetic fertilizers, pesticides, herbicides, fungicides, or GMO seeds, just like organic farms.
- Organic (from the USDA National Organic Program) is a labeling term that indicates that that the food or other agricultural product has been produced through approved methods that integrate cultural, biological, and mechanical practices that foster cycling of resources, promote ecological balance, and conserve biodiversity. Synthetic fertilizers, sewage sludge, irradiation, and genetic engineering may not be used.
- Wild crafted seeds are from crops that include any plant or portion of a plant that is harvested from a growing site that is not conventionally maintained. The land that a wild crop is grown on may not be cultivated by growers and may not be under other agricultural management. An organic wild crop must be harvested in such a way that preserves the natural environment in which the plant grows. And an organic wild crop cannot be gathered from an area that has been exposed to prohibited substances, such as pesticides or chemical fertilizers. Products made with wild crops include essential oils, teas, herbal supplements, and other plant-based products. Sometimes wild seeds are harvested from wild crops as well.

Seed Saving

Before you save seeds from your garden, consider these issues:

- Know how your plants were pollinated: by wind, insect, or self-pollinated.
- Seed from self-pollinated crops are most likely to come true from the parent. (Come true means the new plant will be just like the parent plant.)
- Biennial crops do not produce seed the first year.
- Hybrids do not come true, and attempts at saving them may even be illegal.

Self-pollinated vegetables include beans, lettuces, peas, and tomatoes. Among the vegetable seeds most easily saved are those from nonhybrid tomatoes, peppers, beans, eggplants, cucumbers, summer squash, and watermelons. Generally, all hybrid seedlings and plants are labeled with the term "hybrid" or "F1" on the plant tag. Hybrid seed names may also have a multiplication sign (×) in them to denote that they are a cross between two other varieties. Collect seeds from the fully mature, ripe fruit of these plants.

Tomato seeds are naturally encased in a gelatinous coating that prevents them from sprouting inside the tomato. To save tomato seeds, you need to remove this coating by fermenting them, which mimics the natural rotting of the fruit and has the added bonus of killing any seed-borne tomato disease. To ferment the seeds, squeeze the seeds from a fully ripe fruit into a bowl, add water, and let stand at room temperature for about 3 days. Once fermentation occurs, mold forms on the surface of the water. Add more water, stir, and then gently scrape off the mold and debris from the top. Repeat this water-stir-scraping process until only clean seed remains. Strain, rinse, and leave the seeds at room temperature until they are thoroughly dry.

Pepper seeds should be saved from a fully mature red pepper (green bell peppers are immature and not ripe). Remove the seeds from the fruit cavity and scrape them onto a plate. Let the seeds dry in a non-humid, shaded place, at room temperature until completely dry. Beans, peas, and other legumes should be left in their pods on the plant until they are "rattle dry." Pick the pods and remove the seeds when completely dry.

For eggplant, leave it on the plant until it is well past the stage when you would pick it for kitchen purposes. Eggplants ready for seed saving will be dull, off-colored, and hard. Cut the eggplant in half and pull the flesh away from the seeded area. Let the seeds dry at room temperature.

Cucumbers will change color after they ripen and become mushy. Cut the fruit in half and scrape the seeds into a mesh colander or sieve. Remove their slimy coating by rubbing them gently around the inside of the sieve while washing them. Rinse and dry.

Summer squash seeds should be harvested when the squash is actually too mature to eat. You should not be able to dent the squash skin with your fingernail. Cut it open, scrape the seeds into a bowl, and wash, drain, and dry them.

Watermelon seeds can be removed from the flesh and put in a strainer. Wash them with some water and a drop of dishwashing liquid to remove any sugar from the seeds. Dry thoroughly.

BEST PRACTICES FOR SEED SAVING

BEST CHOICES	GOOD CHOICES	AVOID
Saved from your garden	Regionally grown seeds	Industrial (F1) hybrids
Locally grown seeds saved by other gardeners	Open pollinated	Treated seeds
Nonhybrid	Nonhybrid	GMO seeds (genetically modified)
Heirloom	Heirloom	Industrially produced seeds from large corporate seed companies
Organic	Organic	
Certified naturally grown	Certified naturally grown	
Wild crafted	Wild crafted or organic hybrids	

Label your seed packets or jars with the variety, the date, and where it was grown. Store in a cool, dark, dry place; a refrigerator is a good choice. Avoid opening the container until you are ready to plant. See the chart for seed life and viability in the January chapter. To keep seeds alive and, therefore, productive, it is necessary to keep them viable. This is best done by replanting them from year to year.

Frosts

Knowing what kinds of frosts will occur and when in your area is very helpful to the home gardener. The first and last frost dates for areas within our region are given on page 14. There are three types of frosts that affect your garden:

- at 36°F, a light frost
- at 32°F, a frost/freeze
- at 28°F, a killing frost

SKILL SET

RIPENING TOMATOES

Recall the old wives' tales about vine-ripened tomatoes being the best? Well, that's the truth. But a second-best and season-extending way of enjoying them is to be able to protect those last-of-season not-quite-ripe tomatoes. As the temperatures start to dip, the tomatoes will stop ripening. There just aren't enough hours of daylight or heat in the air to keep them turning red, orange, yellow, or purple. You can create a ripening cupboard or space, i.e., something larger than the kitchen counter or windowsill. Gather several wide, shallow cardboard boxes (the tops of printer paper boxes are ideal). Line them with a couple of layers of newspaper. Collect tomatoes that have turned at least half ripe, and place them carefully, top down, with a bit of space between them, in a single layer in the box, with the final top layer exposed. Putting them in the sunlight is fine, and putting an apple or two in each box is helpful, because apples emit methane gas in small quantities that speeds up the ripening of green tomatoes. As the tomatoes ripen, turn them in the box. You can attempt to ripen totally green tomatoes in the same fashion, but I've found they are better off cooked up into fried green tomatoes or the smallest ones turned into a snazzy pickled substitute for martini olives.

·OCTOBER·

THAT'S A WRAP!

Come October, most of us are ready to put the garden to bed for a while. Sure, we still have fresh herbs, salad greens, glorious squash, and some root crops at hand. But the heat of summer is behind us and we can actually catch our breath. The low light of autumn highlights the bright orange of the pumpkins, the gold butternut squash, and the whole world takes on a soft, warm glow. It's a time to savor the abundance of your growing year. Stalks of corn make festive harvest decorations. The unforgettable fragrance of rhubarb and cinnamon permeates our senses and will carry us through the dim days of winter in pies, sauces, and chutneys.

TO DO THIS MONTH

PLAN

- Think about adding to your garden space next season.
- Make note of the winners and losers: which varieties performed abundantly?
- Save seeds from late-harvest vegetables such as squash, gourds, pumpkins.

PREPARE AND MAINTAIN

- If you have an automated sprinkler system, prepare it for the winter.
- Keep cool-weather crops (newly planted cabbages, onions, lettuces) thinned and properly watered. Cover if necessary on cold nights.
- Mulch, mulch, mulch. Leave the roots of beans and pea plants in the soil, so their nitrogen nodules can enrich the soil. Compost the vines and leaves.
- Discard the vines of cucumbers and summer squash. They may be contaminated with mildew or other diseases.
- Check pumpkins and squash, and turn them or elevate them on twigs or cardboard to keep them from rotting on the bottom.
- Keep adding organic lawn clippings to the compost pile. Keep it turned.

TO DO THIS MONTH ...CONTINUED

SOW AND PLANT

ZONES 3 AND 4

- Plant garlic cloves now before the soil freezes.
- As the frost settles in, there is little to be planted outside in the garden. Gather your seeds and equipment for windowsill gardens.
- Dig and store all root crops—parsnips, carrots, kohlrabi—before the ground freezes solid.

ZONES 5 TO 7

- Sow spinach seeds so they are already in the ground the moment the soil warms next spring.

HARVEST

- Broccoli
- Brussels sprouts
- Cabbage
- Carrots
- Cauliflower
- Corn (a few final ears)
- Garlic
- Herbs (hearty ones like oregano, rosemary, thyme)
- Onions
- Potatoes
- Pumpkins
- Raspberries (late bearing)
- Squash (winter)
- Sunflower seeds

Pumpkins and Squashes

One of the most amazing garden accomplishments is growing a giant pumpkin. While most of us won't be in it to win it with a half-ton (or larger) behemoth, we still love the idea that a seed the size of our little fingernail can yield a pumpkin the size of a vw Bug. Following are some of the record pumpkin weights from our region, sure to be bested in years to come:

Alberta 1,199 pounds
Colorado, 1,308
Idaho, 1,100
Montana, 893
Nevada 715
Oregon 1,610
Saskatchewan 724
Utah, 1,600
Washington, 1,505
Wyoming, 1,012

Pumpkins and squash are in the same family, and in fact, all pumpkins are squash but are distinguished by the fact they are generally orange, round, and edible. Each variety has different criteria for ripeness. A good rule of thumb is to keep track of the data on the original seed package: "days to maturity," size, and color. Butternut squash will morph from gold to tan, and acorn squash will develop a telltale yellow spot on their dark green skin where they are resting on the ground that indicates maturity. You will *not* be able to puncture the rind with your fingernail. The vines will start to deteriorate as the fruit continues to mature.

All winter squash should be harvested after the first light frost in your growing area. To harvest, cut them from the vine leaving a 3- to 4-inch stem on each squash. Cutting the stem too short or breaking it off could cause rotting and mold problems during winter storage. Most of our growing area is dry, but if there is a lot of moisture in the air or the squash are muddy, you should wipe them down with an inexpensive, bacteria-prohibiting wash. Mix 1 gallon of cool water with 1 or 2 tablespoons of white vinegar. Dip your cloth in the solution, wring it out until it's almost dry, then wipe off any debris.

Pumpkins and squash have a firm rind, but they still benefit from curing, the process that allows the rinds to harden for winter storage. After cutting them from the vine, dry them in the sun for a few days, or in a secure spot where raccoons and other pests can't get at them, like a warm garage, covered patio, porch, or barn. Allowing them to dry-cure in a well-ventilated area for up to 20 days will increase their sugar content and prolong their storage life. Store in a cool but not cold, dry, secure place with good air circulation.

Sunflowers

If you grew sunflowers for the seeds, the first of October is the latest you can wait to harvest them. With a friend acting as safety support, and using a stable stepladder, carefully climb up with a sharp knife, saw, or lopping sheers and cut the seed head from the plant, keeping a 12-inch piece of stem on the flower. With the mesh bags still intact, hang the heads to dry in the garage or set the giant flower heads someplace to dry—a place with good air circulation, which is essential. When the seeds start to loosen, rub a cloth over the seed head to dislodge the seeds, letting them fall into a box or onto newspaper.

TIP *In the milder parts of our region, some vegetables can be left in the ground to overwinter. They may have been seeded late in the growing season, and have yet to germinate, or they may be mature and can be kept in the ground until they are needed. Arugula, beets, carrots, kale, and onions fall into this category. Spinach is a crop that can be seeded now and left to germinate on its own time.*

Planting Garlic

Garlic is one of the easiest edibles to grow. I recommend that you purchase certified seed garlic for planting. Seed garlic is actually just a bulb of garlic that you will separate into cloves and plant. The USDA monitors and certifies garlic seed growers to ensure a continuing seed supply of high-quality, disease free, productive garlic varieties. In Idaho and eastern Oregon, your bulbs and seed stock for onions, garlic, leeks, chives, shallots, and potatoes must be state certified as free from white rot. Be extremely cautious when purchasing sets (bulbs) and seed potatoes from sources outside these states. This important rule is to prevent the spread of white rot, a fungal disease that is devastating to these crops. Once in the soil, the fungus can last for thirty years. These crops, when grown from actual seed, do not need certification, but they will take longer to mature, often a year or more.

Soft-neck varieties can be braided together and are less fussy about soil; hard-necked garlic are better "keepers" but demand excellent soil drainage while growing. (A good keeper is a vegetable or fruit that has the potential for a long storage life, be it in a root cellar, garage, or other optimal storage situation. Squash, onions, and apples are good keepers, for instance.) Grow a little of both. Different varieties come in different sizes and so will the seed garlic. Seed garlic may cost as much as $20 per pound, but each pound of seed will yield as much as 4 to 12 pounds of harvested garlic.

A few days before planting the garlic, separate the cloves from the basal plate of the bulb, or the bottom of the bulb where the roots grow, and let them sit so the ends can dry out or cure a bit. Plant each seed 2 inches deep, 4 inches apart, root end down, and pointed end up. Apply 1 or 2 inches of organic compost as mulch. Water in well, and walk away. The garlic will be up in the spring.

SKILL SET

CREATE YOUR OWN COMPOST

Compost is one of the single most beneficial amendments you can add to your garden. You can make it at home, for free. Anything you compost is kept out of the landfill, reducing greenhouse gas emissions and at the same time making a free, organic supplement for your garden soil.

Layering grass clippings and vegetable kitchen scraps, even shredded newspaper, creates a compost pile, and soon, you'll have your very own organic "black gold" for the garden.

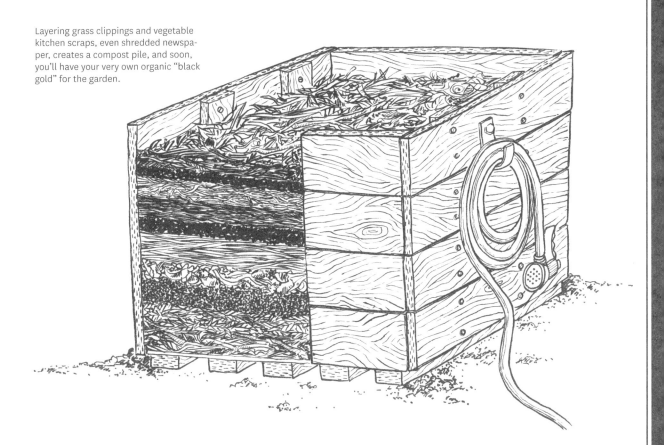

The primary chemical- and pesticide-free elements of a compost pile are:

- browns—dead leaves, branches, and twigs.
- greens—grass clippings, vegetable waste, fruit scraps, and coffee grounds.
- water—sprinkled on the pile from time to time to stimulate the decomposition process.

Your compost pile should have an equal amount of browns to greens. You should also alternate layers of organic materials of different-sized particles: the fine blades of lawn clippings, the cracked bits of eggshells, the wilted leaves of salad greens. The brown materials provide carbon for your compost, the green materials provide nitrogen, and the water provides moisture to help break down the organic matter.

To establish a compost pile, gather up dried leaves, shredded nonglossy paper, eggshells, and clean straw (brown materials) and a lesser amount of fresh kitchen trimmings (fruit rinds, vegetable trimmings). Once your compost pile is established, mix grass clippings and green waste into the pile and bury vegetable and fruit waste under 10 inches of compost material. Carbon and nitrogen, in a ratio of 25:1 (25 carbon/brown, 1 nitrogen/green), will aid in the production of compost. Bacteria, fungi, and microorganisms need carbon and protein to grow and decompose the materials in the pile. Don't worry about exact ratios. When the material at the bottom is dark and rich in color, your compost is ready to use. During the warmer months, compost may be ready in a couple of months. In cooler climates and during the winter months, it will take much longer.

Situate your compost pile or bin in a dry, shady spot near your vegetable garden if possible. You will want to locate it in a long-term, acceptable spot—in other words, not where any odors or the appearances of the pile would be offensive to you or your neighbors.

Do not add leaves or twigs from black walnut trees, coal, charcoal or fireplace ashes, dairy products except for eggshells, diseased plants, fats or oils, animal or meat scraps or waste. Black walnuts contain a chemical that inhibits plant growth. Meat scraps and waste are fatty and will give off a nasty odor. Sometimes furry critters are attracted to fresh food scraps in the compost pile. To deter them, bury the fresh bits at least 8 inches deep in the pile, and put a piece of screen or wire mesh on top of the pile, weighing it down with a couple of rocks. Closed, tumbling compost devices are a good alternative, too.

TAKING STOCK,
TUCKING AWAY

There is so much to be thankful for this month. You've got tasty herb cubes in the freezer, big orange pumpkins eager to be made into holiday pies, and jars of piquant pickles and sweet jams on the pantry shelf. Isn't it wonderful to spend some time just reflecting on the growing year gone by? With just a little bit more tidying up, you will be ready for the quiet season of the gardening year.

TO DO THIS MONTH

PLAN

- Based on your notes for crop rotation, plan where to plant peas and spinach next spring.
- Give away excess squash, pumpkins, and other good keepers to cherished friends.
- Tuck away the seeds, purchased and saved, for next season. Label carefully.
- Order seeds for microgreens.

PREPARE AND MAINTAIN

- Clean an area in preparation for planting spring peas and spinach, and rake in a layer of compost if needed.
- Bring potted chives, rosemary, and parsley plants indoors.
- Make leaf mulch.
- Clean up the garden, removing spent vines and stalks.
- Leave a handful of berries on the bushes for our feathered friends. Pick up any fruit from the ground so it doesn't attract rodents.
- Do a weekly check of produce stored for the winter. Remove any diseased fruits or vegetables.

TO DO THIS MONTH ...CONTINUED

SOW AND PLANT

- Plant any remaining seed garlic.
- Plant spinach seeds in the prepared bed.
- Indoors, plant a container of microgreen seeds and put in strong, warm light.

HARVEST

- Arugula
- Asian greens
- Beets
- Broccoli
- Brussels sprouts
- Cabbage
- Carrots
- Kale
- Leeks
- Microgreens (indoor windowsill)
- Onions
- Parsley
- Parsnips
- Rosemary
- Sage
- Scallions
- Shallots

A Time for Thanksgiving

November is a month of shortening days and long, quiet nights near the hearth. Make up a big pot of soup incorporating some of your hearty root vegetables and pungent herbs. The sun creeps up over the horizon about 8 a.m. and seems to set not many hours later—in the northernmost parts of Idaho and Montana, it sets as early as 5 p.m. The brisk mornings and damp, cold afternoons keep us snuggled up indoors, many of us hoping the ski hills open by Thanksgiving. Brilliant aspen leaves twirl to the ground, the smell of a fire in the fireplace warms the home, and somewhere, someone is baking something delicious with pumpkin and spices. If Mother Nature is in a really good mood, that first hard frost—maybe even the first snow—could be followed by an Indian summer of 75°F days and golden light that paints a remarkable landscape picture. The garden is most likely empty except for a couple of small areas with row covers and cane fruits. A nice clean slate, just daring us to start thinking, What goes where next year? The gardener's mind is like that. There is always next season, next spring, next summer. We are eternal optimists.

Remember to record this year's successes and the few, if any, failures, and start conjuring up ideas for that new planting bed. Or two. Or three. And taking inventory is always a good thing to do. Check back over your inventories of stored fruits and vegetables, as well as the shelves of preserves and food in the freezer. By taking good notes now, you will have a better idea of what you will want or need to grow next year.

Rake leaves away from the trees in your yard, then mow over them to shred them, and apply them to the garden, where needed, as mulch. Leaf mulch is especially useful for protecting strawberry plants.

TIP *Keep a clipboard in the kitchen with a preprinted checklist. Have spaces for freezer items, canned and preserved items, fruits, and squash and root crops in dry storage. Filling out the checklist is the perfect project for a cold afternoon.*

If you've planted a spinach bed, water it in and let it rest until spring. Herbs can be brought in from the garden now. Transplant them into roomy pots with good drainage. They will need a bright, sunny window to flourish.

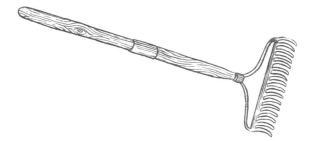

Make sure your rake is in good condition before putting it away for winter.

On a warm afternoon in November, take the opportunity to put the garden beds to bed properly. Clean up and remove any remaining tired, languishing plants that are done producing. If you had insect problems, discard those plants; if not, they can be put in the compost pile. You'll be glad you did.

Tend Your Tools

November is also the time to clean and maintain all indispensable garden tools you've been using this season. Keeping your tools in good condition will prolong their usefulness and keep them in top working order.

I suggest gathering all your garden tools together in one place. I lay mine out on the driveway, the lawn, or on a tarp where I can eyeball each item carefully. Clean each tool thoroughly. Hose off any dirt from the blades of the shovel and trowels. Wipe down the handles. Inspect wooden handles for splinters or loose shafts. Make sure to attend to any tools that need repairs. Sharpen all the blades of your pruning shears, loppers, and gardener's knife. A dose of WD-40 or other lubricant will keep the mechanisms on your cutting devices working smoothly. Shovel blades can be sharpened too. A lawn mower blade repair/sharpening shop is a good place to have this done. Make sure everything is clean and dry before you put it away for the winter. Carefully stow your tools for next year in a clean, dry place.

With a helper, shake out and neatly fold or roll up the row cover material and stash it for next spring. You may want to leave a portion of row cover or horticultural fleece in place to protect the last vestiges of growing edibles. While the garden naturally becomes dormant from now until late February, there may be some small, vigorous greens still growing; encouraged by the warmth of a heat retaining wall and sunny Indian summer days. I've known gardeners who were still harvesting small greens in December, which is entirely possible if the winter is mild.

If you've not had your sprinkler system winterized, do so now. If you have an expensive, complicated, timed irrigation system, it is advisable to have it "blown out" by a company that specializes in this process. They have the equipment to remove all water from the system. This will prevent water in the pipes from freezing and bursting the pipes during a cold winter.

If your system is not complicated, and if you are sure you can drain all the water from the system, you can do the task yourself:

- Turn off the water to the irrigation system at the main valve.
- Set the automatic irrigation controller to the "rain" setting.
- Turn on each of the valves to release pressure in the pipes.
- Drain all of the water out of any irrigation components that might freeze.
- Drain hoses and sprayers, and put them away. Keep one hose out and handy for occasional deep watering but disconnect it from the outside water faucet, so the hose bib won't freeze and damage your household water pipes.

Remaining Garden Tasks

Here's hoping you are making the most of your home-grown compost piles, and manure and comfrey teas. But if you do have any bottled, boxed, or bagged soil amendments in the shed, carefully seal and retire them to a cool, dry storage area. Make sure they are properly labeled, and don't store them near a furnace or heating system.

If you have planted microgreens for your windowsill, the zesty greens are ready in as few as 5 days. Snip as you go, and enjoy the crunch and flavor in salads and sandwiches. These fresh autumn greens are a special treat. Use any container—a seed-starting tray or a plastic salad clamshell is perfect. Fill the bottom with 1 to 2 inches of good seed-starting mix, dampen gently, scatter the seed over the top, cover with ⅛ inch of the starting mix, and dampen again. Do not let the container dry out, but don't let it drown. Use small scissors to harvest the green sprouts when they are 1 to 2 inches tall. Plant another box in a week to ensure a constant supply of fresh greens.

If you had problems growing plants in any particular area of your garden and cannot figure out the cause, this is a good time to get a soil test done for that area. You will have plenty of time to apply recommended nutrients to the garden before spring planting.

MAKING A COLD FRAME

To have seedlings ready early for next year, consider making a cold frame—the simplest mini greenhouse ever.

A cold frame will let you start seeds outdoors earlier than cold temperatures would normally allow, set out small transplants, and give plants a measure of protection from unpredictable spring or late autumn cold snaps.

The cold frame is a simple box ("frame") with a lid. Before making the box, find an old glass window to use as the cover. Or, you can create a cover by making a frame of lightweight wood and stapling a piece of heavy-duty opaque plastic sheeting over it. Using lumber that is at least 1 inch thick and 12 inches wide, build a bottomless box to match the size of the cover or window.

The box should be manageable and, ideally, moveable. The smallest cold frames can be picked up and put away or dismantled and stored when they aren't needed, so I recommend building your frame to be 2 by 3 feet or 4 by 4 feet. You can even use 4 bales of hay or straw for the sides or walls, if you can get those. The thickness of the hay bales provides great insulation, and the frame is easily removed when not in service. Place the cold frame in the garden where it will get sun, ideally a southern exposure, so it can capture the life-giving solar power when the ground is still frozen and the ambient air is too chilly for putting transplants out in the ground. Once the vegetables sprout and begin to grow, if you have a glass lid, open it on moderate, sunny days so the young plants won't burn.

·DECEMBER·

GARDEN
GIFTS

In the Rockies, across the sagebrush steppe and high desert areas, winter offers crystal blue skies, snow flurries or drifts, short days, and long nights. Across the region, from Boise to Butte to Bountiful, the ground is likely frozen now. Moving toward the shortest day of the year, the Winter Solstice, Mother Nature takes a well-earned break from the gaudy colors of the growing seasons and slips into peaceful repose, often under a quiet white blanket of snow.

TO DO THIS MONTH

PLAN

- Order unusual and popular seeds for gift giving (and for your garden) as soon as possible.

PREPARE AND MAINTAIN

- Protect overwintering root vegetables and other edibles from frost with cold frames, hay bales, and horticultural fleece.
- If your garden is not already under a thermal blanket of snow, water cane fruits deeply this month. Once is enough.
- Inspect potatoes, squash, carrots, and other edibles in dry storage. Remove any with soft spots or signs of decay.
- Dig and store all root crops—parsnips, carrots, kohlrabi—before the ground freezes solid.
- Locate a juniper shrub—one you know is chemical free. Harvest the frosty blue berries for spice sachets.

TO DO THIS MONTH ...CONTINUED

SOW AND PLANT

- Every five to ten days, or as needed, start another fresh indoor tray of tasty microgreens.

HARVEST

- Brussels sprouts
- Cabbage
- Kale
- Microgreens
- Parsley
- Rosemary
- Rutabagas
- Sage
- Thyme

For the gift-giving season and festive meals of this time of year, nothing beats a thoughtful gift from the garden or for the garden for your favorite gardener. Charitable gifts to your local botanical garden are greatly appreciated. And don't forget to make donations of extra seed, tools, gloves, hoses, sprayers, and gift certificates to community gardens. They are often in great need of supplies to do their good work growing food for those without gardens.

Gifts, Grown and Sown

I like to think of garden gifts in two categories: those that are grown and those that can be sown.

Here's a partial list of holiday gifts you might give, using edibles from your garden:

- Dried mint leaves in a jar or handmade mint tea bags for tea.
- Rosemary cheese crackers for holiday parties.
- Fruit jams, compotes, preserves, and chutneys.
- Pickled beets, cucumbers, asparagus, green beans, green tomatoes, or vegetable giardiniera—a mix of pickled onions, cauliflower, carrots, peppers, and celery.
- Lavender sachets.
- Saved seeds in packets.
- Juniper berries, rosemary, and dried onion spice mix for pork roasts.
- Roasted, salted sunflower or pumpkin seeds.
- Walla Walla onion dip mix: Combine dried Walla Walla (or any other mild onion) pieces with dried parsley, chives, a bit of salt and pepper for mixing with yogurt or sour cream.

- Frozen cubes of preserved herbs in olive oil.
- Frozen rhubarb simple syrup for holiday drinks, rhubarb-tinis, or rhubarb punch. The mega doses of vitamin C in the rhubarb juice are especially welcome during cold and flu season.
- Corn relish for festive antipasto platters.

Clever, simple packaging can make the most humble, heartfelt gifts a work of art. Hand-letter your gift tags for the jam jars. Use inexpensive raffia or red and white butchers' twine for tying brown craft paper–wrapped gifts. Using pinking shears or craft scissors, cut out festive rounds or squares of fabric for covering jam jar lids, leaving a bit to hang below the "jar ring." Include your recipe as a part of the package.

Gifts that are "sown" are gifts of seeds or tools. Make your own seed packages and stamp or draw the corresponding vegetable image on the packet. Give gifts of your favorite garden tools, to encourage the growth of a new gardener or even an experienced one. One of the most memorable gifts I've ever received came from a fellow gardener: a packet of 'Lazy Housewife' heirloom bean seeds. The name of the beans made me laugh out loud. In the spring I grew those seeds into beans and thought of her when I planted, tended, harvested, and ate them. Today, the red and white twine and seed envelope with her drawing serves as a book mark in one of my favorite gardening books.

Seed catalogs along with holiday gift catalogs fill your mailbox to overflowing this month. Take a tip from the established seed companies and create your own special planting collections. If you have saved the seeds yourself, all the better. If not, no worries; combine store or catalog-bought varieties. Some ideas:

- A salad bowl garden includes seeds for a variety of lettuces: green, red, romaine, speckled, ruffled, and smooth.
- A stir-fry garden includes seeds for bell peppers, green onions, and Asian greens like bok choy and tatsoi.
- A salsa garden would include seeds for onions, heirloom tomatoes, hot and mild peppers, parsley, and cilantro.
- The "herbalicious" collection might have parsley, dill, chives, cilantro, and mint seeds.
- The Three Sisters Garden is the historical, traditional planting combination made famous by the Plains and Southwestern Indian tribes. It includes heirloom seeds for pole beans, corn, and squash. Include the memorable history of this planting method with complete instructions.

Another idea is to give a gift certificate to your favorite gardener or gardeners for a selection of special cane fruits or fancy Mara des Bois strawberries to be delivered at the proper planting time. Include a note recommending they order immediately for best selection.

Don't forget the luxury list of gifts to give (or receive!). Include anything your friend (or you) might not buy on her own.

- A pair of perfect, well-made, precision pruners and a sharpening kit.
- A traditional wooden trug, or garden basket, or a colorful garden tote for produce.
- A sturdy tool kit or cart for organizing rakes, shovels, spades, and trowels.
- A pair or several pairs of your favorite gardening gloves.

- One or more books for beginning or adding to a garden library—hers or yours!
- A gift certificate for helping your friend to build and plant a raised bed.
- A gift of a reliable gardening service for a season, for someone you know who may not be able to tend her garden as often as she would like. Most communities now have talented, knowledgeable vegetable gardeners available to hire. They will plant, tend, maintain, and harvest your garden for you for a fee.
- A year's membership in a csa, for someone without the space for a garden. Community Supported Agriculture programs are available in almost every town in our region. Generally, you purchase a subscription to a local farmer's organic garden, and once a week during the growing season, you either pick up your share of produce or it is delivered to you. csa subscriptions may include also options such as fresh eggs, freshly cut flowers, herbs, honey, and homegrown grains or flours.
- A canning and preserving starter kit: include a canning pot, the insets for lifting jars, hot pads, tongs, a canning recipe and instruction book, plus a case of canning jars and lids. Maybe also add labels and a waterproof marker for labeling the jars.
- You might consider giving a gardener friend a certificate for a manicure. And any gardener would like a day-spa package including a massage for those sore muscles.

Sharing the garden's bounty carries the spirit of gardening well into the New Year. May your gardens be colorful, peaceful, and abundant.

SKILL SET

GIFTS FOR THE BIRDS

Don't forget to leave a holiday treat for our feathered friends. Using a needle and thread, create simple strings of juniper berries, popped popcorn, or dried berries. Or wrap an apple tightly with string, spread peanut butter around the outside, and then roll it in sunflower seeds. These items can be hung from tree branches in the garden, and you'll have fun watching them feast!

EDIBLES
A TO Z

PLANTING AND HARVESTING CHART
ZONES 3 & 4

Planting
Harvesting

These charts list the planting and harvesting dates in the mountain states region for annual plants cultivated outdoors in the garden without protective devices. The dates in the charts are approximate. Soil and air temperatures of your particular garden will affect germination and maturity dates of edibles. You'll find more information about starting seeds indoors, and which vegetables to direct sow or transplant, in the profiles of specific vegetables.

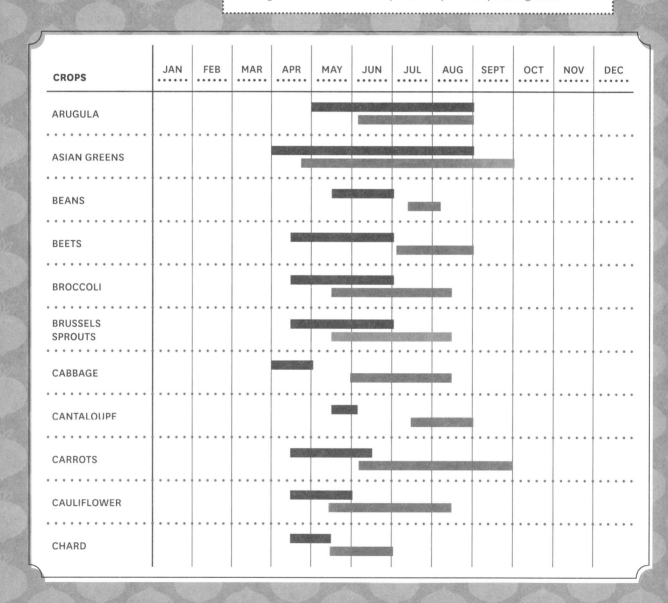

CROPS	JAN	FEB	MAR	APR	MAY	JUN	JUL	AUG	SEPT	OCT	NOV	DEC
ARUGULA												
ASIAN GREENS												
BEANS												
BEETS												
BROCCOLI												
BRUSSELS SPROUTS												
CABBAGE												
CANTALOUPE												
CARROTS												
CAULIFLOWER												
CHARD												

CROPS	JAN	FEB	MAR	APR	MAY	JUN	JUL	AUG	SEPT	OCT	NOV	DEC
COLLARDS				▬	▬	▬						
CORN					▬	▬	▬	▬				
CUCUMBERS					▬		▬	▬				
EGGPLANT						▬	▬	▬				
GARLIC							▬			▬		
KALE					▬	▬	▬	▬	▬			
KOHLRABI				▬		▬						
LEEKS				▬	▬			▬	▬			
LETTUCE					▬	▬	▬	▬	▬			
MUSTARD GREENS					▬	▬	▬	▬	▬	▬		
ONIONS, BULB					▬		▬	▬				
ONIONS, GREEN				▬	▬		▬	▬				
PARSNIPS					▬			▬	▬			
PEAS, GARDEN AND SNAP				▬	▬	▬	▬					
PEPPERS						▬		▬	▬			

ZONES 3 & 4 ...CONTINUED

Planting
Harvesting

CROPS	JAN	FEB	MAR	APR	MAY	JUN	JUL	AUG	SEPT	OCT	NOV	DEC
POTATOES				██	██		▓▓	▓				
RADISHES				██	██	▓▓▓▓						
RUTABAGAS					██		▓▓▓▓	▓	▓			
SHALLOTS			██				▓▓	▓▓▓	▓			
SPINACH				██		▓▓▓▓	▓	██ ▓	▓			
SQUASH, SUMMER						██		▓▓▓	▓			
SQUASH (WINTER) AND PUMPKINS						██			▓▓			
TOMATOES					██	▓▓	▓▓▓	▓▓				
TURNIPS				██		▓▓		██		▓▓		
WATERMELONS					██			▓▓				

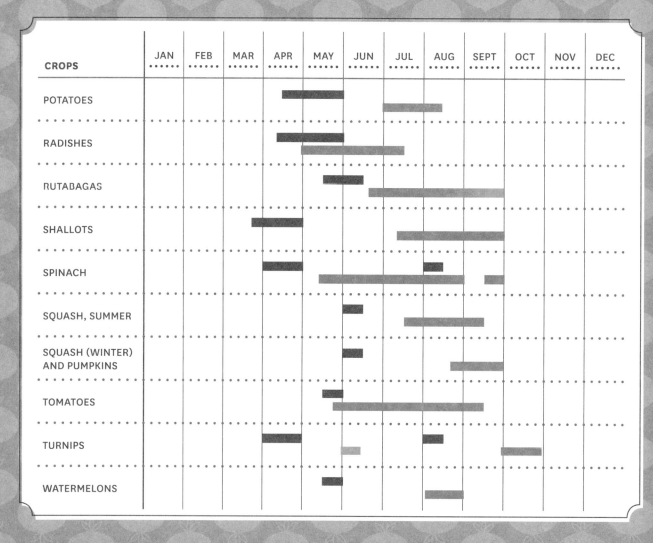

PLANTING AND HARVESTING CHART
ZONES 5 & 6

Planting
Harvesting

These charts list the planting and harvesting dates in the mountain states region for annual plants cultivated outdoors in the garden without protective devices. The dates in the charts are approximate. Soil and air temperatures of your particular garden will affect germination and maturity dates of edibles. You'll find more information about starting seeds indoors, and which vegetables to direct sow or transplant, in the profiles of specific vegetables.

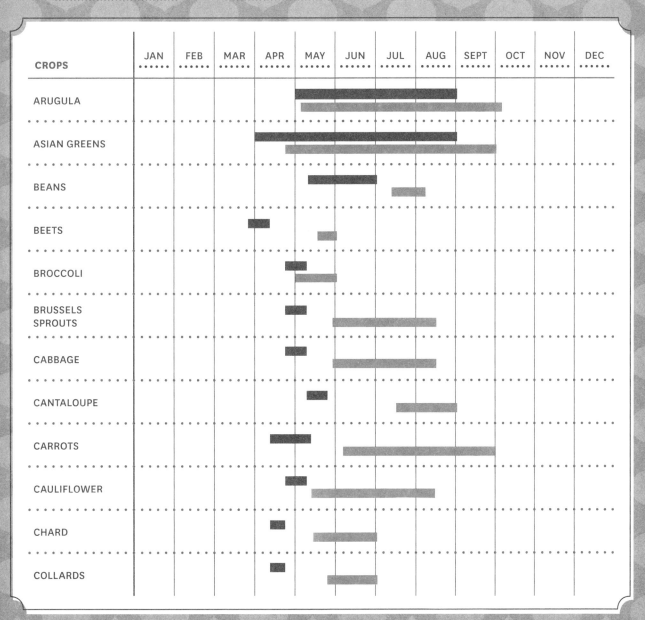

CROPS	JAN	FEB	MAR	APR	MAY	JUN	JUL	AUG	SEPT	OCT	NOV	DEC
ARUGULA					Planting (May–Aug) / Harvesting (May–Oct)							
ASIAN GREENS			Planting (Mar–Aug) / Harvesting (May–Sept)									
BEANS					Planting (May–Jun)		Harvesting (Jul–Aug)					
BEETS			Planting (Mar–Apr)		Harvesting (May–Jun)							
BROCCOLI				Planting (Apr)	Harvesting (Apr–Jun)							
BRUSSELS SPROUTS				Planting (Apr)		Harvesting (Jun–Aug)						
CABBAGE				Planting (Apr)		Harvesting (Jun–Aug)						
CANTALOUPE				Planting (May)			Harvesting (Jul–Sept)					
CARROTS				Planting (Apr–May)		Harvesting (Jun–Oct)						
CAULIFLOWER				Planting (Apr)	Harvesting (May–Aug)							
CHARD				Planting (Apr)	Harvesting (May–Jul)							
COLLARDS				Planting (Apr)		Harvesting (Jun–Jul)						

ZONES 5 & 6 ...CONTINUED

■ Planting
■ Harvesting

CROPS	JAN	FEB	MAR	APR	MAY	JUN	JUL	AUG	SEPT	OCT	NOV	DEC
CORN					▅			▬				
CUCUMBERS					▅		▬▬					
EGGPLANT					▅			▬				
GARLIC							▬			▅		
KALE				▅		▬▬▬▬						
KOHLRABI				▅		▬▬▬						
LEEKS				▅					▬▬▬▬			
LETTUCE				▅▅▅▅▅▅▅▅▅								
MUSTARD GREENS				▅▅▅▅▅		▬▬▬▬						
ONIONS, BULB					▅▅▅▅							
ONIONS, GREEN				▅▅			▬▬					
PARSNIPS				▅				▬▬▬				

CROPS	JAN	FEB	MAR	APR	MAY	JUN	JUL	AUG	SEPT	OCT	NOV	DEC
PEAS, GARDEN			▓	▓		░						
PEPPERS						▓		░	░			
POTATOES			▓	▓			░	░				
RADISHES				▓	▓	▓	░					
RUTABAGAS				▓	▓	░	░	▓		░	░	
SHALLOTS			▓				░	░	░			
SPINACH				▓	░	░	░	░				
SQUASH, SUMMER						▓	░	░	░			
SQUASH (WINTER) AND PUMPKINS						▓			░	░		
TOMATOES					░	▓	░	░	░	░		
TURNIPS				▓		░	░	░				
WATERMELONS						▓		░				

PLANTING AND HARVESTING CHART
ZONE 7

Planting
Harvesting

These charts list the planting and harvesting dates in the mountain states region for annual plants cultivated outdoors in the garden without protective devices. The dates in the charts are approximate. Soil and air temperatures of your particular garden will affect germination and maturity dates of edibles. You'll find more information about starting seeds indoors, and which vegetables to direct sow or transplant, in the profiles of specific vegetables.

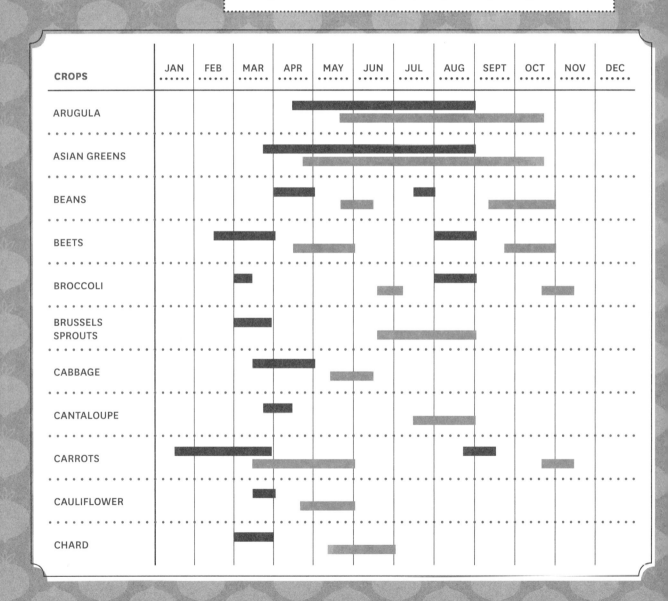

CROPS	JAN	FEB	MAR	APR	MAY	JUN	JUL	AUG	SEPT	OCT	NOV	DEC
ARUGULA												
ASIAN GREENS												
BEANS												
BEETS												
BROCCOLI												
BRUSSELS SPROUTS												
CABBAGE												
CANTALOUPE												
CARROTS												
CAULIFLOWER												
CHARD												

CROPS	JAN	FEB	MAR	APR	MAY	JUN	JUL	AUG	SEPT	OCT	NOV	DEC
COLLARDS			■		▬	▬		■		▬	▬	
CORN				■		▬	▬	▬				
CUCUMBERS				■	■	▬	■ ▬	■	▬	▬	▬	
EGGPLANT				■	■		▬	▬				
GARLIC							▬				■	
KALE			■		▬	▬	▬		■		▬	
KOHLRABI			■		▬	▬						
LEEKS			■	■				▬	▬	▬	▬	
LETTUCE				■	■ ▬	■ ▬	■ ▬	■ ▬	▬	▬	▬	▬
MUSTARD GREENS			■		▬	▬	▬	■	■		▬	▬
ONIONS, BULB			■			▬	▬	▬				
ONIONS, GREEN				■	■		▬	▬				
PARSNIPS			■				▬	▬	▬			
PEAS, GARDEN AND SNAP			■		▬	▬						
PEPPERS				■		▬	▬	▬				

ZONE 7 ...CONTINUED

Planting
Harvesting

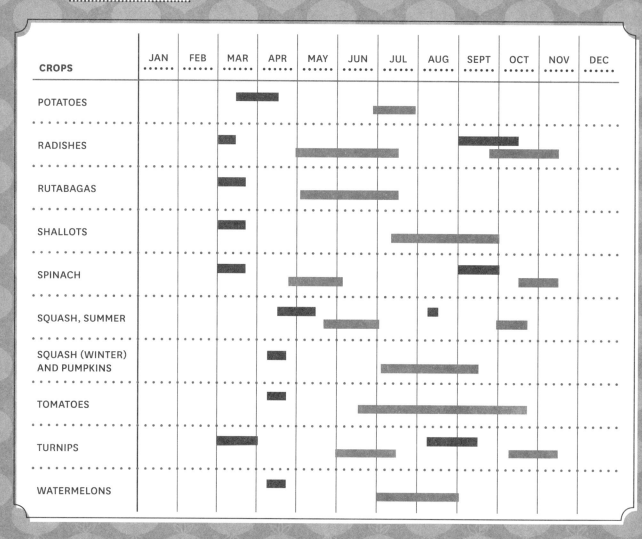

CROPS	JAN	FEB	MAR	APR	MAY	JUN	JUL	AUG	SEPT	OCT	NOV	DEC
POTATOES			■				▬					
RADISHES			■		▬▬▬▬				■■	▬▬		
RUTABAGAS			■■		▬▬▬▬							
SHALLOTS			■■				▬▬▬▬					
SPINACH			■■	▬▬▬					■■		▬▬	
SQUASH, SUMMER				■■	▬▬▬			■		▬		
SQUASH (WINTER) AND PUMPKINS				■			▬▬▬▬					
TOMATOES				■		▬▬▬▬▬▬▬▬						
TURNIPS			■■		▬▬▬			■■		▬▬		
WATERMELONS				■		▬▬▬▬						

Artichokes

A single globe artichoke plant will make a stunning focal point in any garden. If you have room for more than one plant, you could even place them throughout a perennial border. They often reach 5 feet in height, and their fuzzy, silvery, deeply lobed leaves and cap-tivating periwinkle buds are spectacular. The plant resembles the not-so-appreciated Canada thistle, but this plant's flower buds are meant to be savored. Originally from the Mediterranean, artichokes do well in our region if given a warm, early start and are not subjected to drought.

GROWING In our region, it is best to procure artichokes from nurseries as seedlings, then transplant them into the garden when daytime soil temperatures have warmed up to a reliable 60 to 65°F (just one reason to purchase that $10 soil thermometer). Give each plant plenty of space,

because that the plant may thrive in that spot for two years before fading. Place artichokes where they will get plenty of sun, 4 to 5 feet apart. Add a generous amount of aged compost to each planting hole, and position each plant in the hole at the same soil level as in its original pot.

Several purple and heirloom varieties are available from seed catalogs. Seedlings need two to three months of growth to reach adequate size for transplants into the garden. Germinate the seeds in a tray, at 70 to 75°F (a warming mat is very useful), then plant the seedlings in small pots. When they are strong and stout and the weather has warmed, then they can be planted out into the garden. The purple varieties produce very tender buds, delicious when harvested and cooked whole at just 2 inches in diameter.

In the garden, some late afternoon shade is fine. Good drainage is essential. Artichokes need at least 2 inches of water per week. Since they are shallow rooted, be careful weeding around established plants. A thick layer of compost or mulch is very helpful. As the buds develop on the stalk, you may want to remove the small lateral buds near the largest bud, which tends to increase the size of the primary bud. If aphids are a nuisance, spray the plant with an organic insecticidal soap.

In the warmest parts of our region, artichokes may winter over, surviving for a second growing season and producing heavily. At the end of each growing season, cut the stalk back to the base of the plant and cover with a thick layer of mulch.

HARVESTING The edible buds are ready to harvest when they are 3 inches in diameter and tightly closed—definitely before the buds open and thistledown starts to appear. Cut the stem 1-½ inches below the base of the bud with a sharp knife. Prepare immediately because the quality of the bud begins to deteriorate as soon as it is removed from the plant.

VARIETIES **Green Globe**, **Imperial Star**, and **Violetta di Chiogga** (all take 110 to 150 days) can be found at most nurseries. Seeds for purple varieties like **Purple of Romagna**, **Violetta Precoce**, and **Violet de Provence** (all 150 to 200 days) can be found online.

Arugula

Arugula. Rockette. Roquette. Rocket. Rucola. All these names are used for this zingy, peppery, tasty green plant. Because of its distinctive flavor, arugula is a perfect fresh leafy green for salads or sandwiches. If you are feeling flush with a surplus of arugula, it can be sautéed. You can pay $5 for a couple of handfuls at the market—barely enough for a two-person salad— or $2.50 will buy you a packet of seeds that will keep you in fresh arugula for a year.

GROWING Direct sow into the garden as soon as the soil is workable. The seeds won't germinate until the soil warms up, but you can plant anyway. Arugula does well in any soil, and is very manageable in a patio pot. Remove ¼ inch of soil from the area to be planted and set that soil aside. Scatter the seeds evenly across the area, at least 2 inches

inch apart. Carefully dust the reserved soil across the top of the seeds. Water in with a gentle spray mist. Keep evenly moist until the first signs of life appear, and then back off on the water. Seeds will germinate in 5 to 10 days.

When the seedlings are about 1 inch high, you can thin them a bit, eating the thinnings out of hand or adding them to an otherwise bland lettuce salad. Allow a few plants to bolt, scattering their seeds, and another crop of arugula will be on its way. Hot weather will cause the plants to bolt quickly. The flowers are edible, too. Plant a few seeds every couple of weeks to keep a fresh crop coming.

HARVESTING Begin harvesting when the leaves are at least 2 inches tall and before they are 6 to 8 inches tall. Arugula can be snipped at the plant's base. I prefer to work my way evenly through the planting area, snipping different plants with a pair of kitchen scissors. Retain a couple of leaves in the center of each plant and new growth will appear in a few days. Often the plants will send up new shoots and you will have a second harvest.

VARIETIES Wild and domestic arugula seeds are available and there is great debate over which is better. The genus *Diplotaxis* is for the wild child; it is reputedly slower to bolt in hot weather. **Sylvetta Wild** (30 to 40 days) is a recommended wild variety. *Eruca sativa* is the cultivated species. Look for **Astro** (38 days) as a flavorful, domestic variety. Find seeds labeled "organic" and "heirloom," if possible.

Asian Greens

Some of the names are hard to pronounce, but all members of this large group of tender greens are quick to grow, tasty and crisp, and perfect in salads or stir-fries. Asian greens is a large category of leafy vegetables of Asian ancestry. They include greens, ribs of leaves, stems of leaves, buds, and pea shoots. A good many of them are in the mustard or cabbage family. These darlings of the produce world are at home in any garden and often overwinter with just a simple row cover as protection from the cold.

GROWING These are so easy to grow, you won't believe it. Start with rich, fertile soil or planting mix, in a well-drained garden bed, or in large flowerpot at least 20 inches in diameter and 9 to 12 inches deep, and scatter the seeds across the planting area. Tamp in gently using the palm of your hand. Water in gently with a fine spray, and cover with a ¼-inch layer of soil or planting mix. Keep the soil barely moist, and the seeds will germinate in as few as 5 days in warm weather or as long as 12 to 14 days in colder weather. When the seedlings are 3 to 4 inches tall, thin to allow about 3 inches around each plant, and eat the thinnings. Snipping just a few leaves with scissors may encourage a second set of leaves.

HARVESTING Most baby Asian greens can be harvested when they are just 3 to 4 inches tall. Baby bok choy and some other Asian greens will be mature and ready to eat when they are no more than 6 inches in height. Check the seed packet for harvest information. Leaves of these greens are tasty up until they show signs of bolting or blooming.

VARIETIES There are almost as many varieties of Asian greens as there are Asian dialects. **Mei Quing Choi**, **Kamatsuma**, **Tatsoi** (21 days for baby, 40 days for mature), and **Mizuna** (5 days for baby, 40 days for mature), as well as blends of all, are easy to find. Mizuna is especially tasty with a bit of zing, and it is a cut-and-come-again green. You will find, too, that the small leaves of edible chrysanthemums, tiny mustard plants, and other miniature members of the cabbage family make good edible greens. The ones with fleshy, thick stems hold up well in a quick sauté.

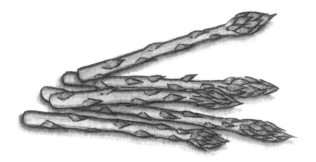

Asparagus

Asparagus is considered a harbinger of spring. When it pops up in the garden, is cut and briefly cooked, and arrives on the dinner table, capped with a splash of olive oil, and a dash of salt and freshly ground pepper, you know spring has sprung. Tender fresh spears are available for such a short time each year, the crop has attained star status when it is in season. Pickled asparagus spears in Bloody Marys are good in any season. Having fresh asparagus at hand in your own garden, and knowing that the asparagus bed will produce for fifteen to twenty years, may thwart any urge you have to move to another house.

GROWING An asparagus bed should be laid out and planted with care and forethought because the "crowns" will serve you handsomely for a very long time. You will be purchasing crowns that have no resemblance to what you envision as asparagus. They are strange little things, resembling small dried up brown octopuses. And yes, they need a couple of years to mature, but asparagus is the plant that keeps on giving. Gorgeous in the flower border, the feathery foliage makes a graceful backdrop for perennial plantings. Asparagus foliage can reach 4 to 5 feet in height. Be sure to cut it back after the frost has turned it brown.

Plant asparagus as soon as the soil is workable in the spring. Asparagus must have good drainage, but other than that, it is not picky about the soil in which it is planted. If possible, start with rich topsoil. There are two planting methods. The newer way—for small gardens and ornamental border plantings—requires that you dig a big hole for each crown, 18 inches deep and at least 18 inches wide. Backfill the hole with aged organic compost—don't use fresh manure or "hot" compost. Mound the compost to within 2 inches of the top of the hole. Place the asparagus crown on the mound, with the roots fanned out like an octopus and down over the sides of the mound. Then cover the crown with 2 inches of soil. On your calendar, make a note to add 2 inches more of soil on top of the crowns in the fall. Water in well, and walk away. The first year, allow the stalks to grow, without picking many of them, giving the crowns time to build their energy and go to seed. You can place additional crowns in successive holes, using the same spacing, the next year.

The older, well-known way of planting asparagus is suited for large garden spaces and long rows. Dig a deep trench, 18 inches deep, allowing 18 inches of space from the center of one crown to the next. Fill the trench with well-composted organic matter, mounding it high in the center.

Crowns are placed on the high point, with the roots dangling down the sides of the mound. Backfill and cover the crowns with 2 inches of soil. Make a note to add 2 inches more of soil in the fall. Again, leave the asparagus alone the first season, and pick only for three weeks the second year.

Asparagus grows quickly during warm days, and especially after a rainy spell. The new spears—picked in the evening, just before dinner—will be at their prime.

HARVESTING Harvest sparingly if at all the first year. Use a sharp knife to cut the spears at ground level. The second year, harvest for a few weeks, leaving about one-quarter of the stalks to go to seed. By the third year, your asparagus plants will be well established and can be harvested for as long as they produce. There are two different thoughts on

the right size for harvesting asparagus. Some people love the spears when they are slender and as round as a pencil. Other folks like them to be ½ inch in diameter. It's up to you. But in both instances, harvest the stalks when they are 6 to 9 inches tall. The new varieties of asparagus will yield up to ½ to ¾ pound of fresh spears per crown. A harvest of 1 pound of asparagus makes a nice side-dish serving for four people. If you love asparagus, plant five or more crowns for each family member. And remember, it will take up to three years for each crown to produce that plentifully.

VARIETIES Look for **Jersey Giant** and **Jersey Knight**, or the royal **Purple Passion**. The old standby is **Martha Washington**, and while nothing is wrong with Martha, the newer varieties tend to be more productive.

Beans

Beans are just so simple to grow in the vegetable garden, in a decorative flower garden, or in a large flowerpot. They look fascinating, twining and climbing their way up a trellis in a pot on the patio. They are nutritious, delicious, and beautiful in any dish. The beans themselves come in a broad range of colorations: violet, gold, speckled, and green.

There are many bean types and growing habits: pole beans, bush beans, dry beans, snap beans, yard-long beans, Italian beans, French filet beans, and many more. You can easily find seeds for the delicious, wide, flat Italian (Romano) pole and bush beans. Many bean types can be grown for dry shelling beans, such as limas. For decorative

purposes, grow Scarlet Runner types: the red beans are edible and the edible vibrant scarlet blossoms are stunning in the garden. I encourage you, my gardener friend, to try all of them. Bush beans tend to come to maturity all at the same time, generally over a two-week period, so for these, just plant a new crop every two weeks. Pole beans mature over a longer period, and tend to be more productive.

Beans grown for drying, such as red beans, kidney beans, lima beans, black beans, are grown just like other beans, but when the plants start to wane and the pods have started drying out, pull the plants up by the roots, hang them together upside down in clumps, and let them dry thoroughly before removing them from the pods. You can wrap the bunch in an old sheet and beat the sheet with a broom to dislodge the beans from their pods. Clean all the debris from the bean seeds, and store in a cool dry place, labeled and dated. They are best eaten in one year.

GROWING Bush beans and pole beans bear the same kind of beans but have different growing habits. Pole beans grow 5 to 6 feet tall and need support: a trellis, a curtain-type structure, or a tepee. Growing them in a tepee format makes a great living playhouse for small children. Pole beans will automatically wrap around their support, but you may need to initially help each vine find the trellis and get going. They will twine clockwise.

For planting bean seeds, wait until the soil is warm. Planting too early can result in rotted bean seeds. Plant the seeds ½ to 1 inch deep in friable, loose soil. Pole beans should be spaced 6 inches apart with supports 6 to 7 feet tall. Space bush beans at least 4 inches apart; they grow to be about 2 feet tall and do not need supports. Water is best applied with a drip system at the base of the plants, because bean leaves are easily damaged and vulnerable to disease if they get too much moisture. Water beans regularly.

Keep an eye out for bean beetles. They are cousins to the ladybug or lady beetle and look similar. They can be identified by their yellow or tan color (versus orange or red) and their 16 black spots. In late spring or early summer, be alert to little yellow spots or "eggs" on the underside of your bean plants' leaves. Remove them if you see them. You can also dust the plants with diatomaceous earth. Wash bean pods thoroughly before eating.

HARVESTING Both bush and pole types of beans are ready to harvest when they are green, somewhat plump, not quite ripe, before the seeds start to swell. Using both hands, snap the bean from the vine just above the cap of the bean. Keep beans harvested so they will continue to produce.

VARIETIES Pole beans: **Hilda Romano** is a quick-producing Romano-type bean, with 8- to 9-inch pods (60 days). **Lazy Housewife** (75 days) is delicious. **Italian Romano** (65 days) and **Kentucky Wonder** and **TriColor** (both 60 days) are excellent choices. Bush beans: **Dragon Tongue** (65 days) is a marvelously streaked, multipurpose, hardworking bean. It can be used as a snap bean or allowed to mature for dried beans. Plants are 2 feet tall. **Nash** (48 to 54 days) is recommended for its incredible productivity. **Kentucky Blue** (65 days), **Royal Burgundy** (60 days), and **Slenderette** (55 days) are favorite bush beans. Dry beans: Some of the best beans for drying have the best names: **Christmas**, **Jacob's Cattle**, **Calypso**, and **Silver Cloud**—allow 90 days for all of these for dried beans.

Beets

This quintessential deeply colored vegetable is enjoying a resurgence in popularity at home and on menus in fancy restaurants. Loaded with antioxidants, beets are very low in calories and high in folate and other essential nutrients. Beet greens are high in beta-carotene and magnesium, and make a tasty addition to soups and stir-fries. Golden beets and striped beets offer different visual appeal and flavors. Beets are delicious roasted in foil, boiled, canned, or pickled. Roasted beets are excellent, sliced for salads and tossed with a delicate, vinegary dressing. Fresh young beets can be grated into a salad for a burst of flavor and color.

GROWING Direct sow seeds into the garden from April to June, or one month before the last frost in your area. You may replant in late July for a fall crop, if your area stays warm enough. Plant seeds ½ to 1 inch deep in loamy soil, spacing the seeds 1 to 2 inches apart, and thinning later seedlings to 3 to 4 inches apart. The thinnings (tops in particular) are delicious and can be used in salads or stir-fries. If planting in a square-foot method, plant 9 seeds per square. Beets do best in full sun, but they will do well with some afternoon shade.

Like any of the other root crops (carrots, turnips, radishes), beets will benefit from a well-worked soil, free of lumps and rocks, so that their foray into the depth of the garden is easy and the resulting crop is uniform and nicely shaped. Water seedlings deeply and regularly to avoid deformed, tough, fibrous beets.

HARVESTING Beets are ready for harvest in about 60 days. Check the root for maturity: the top of the beet should be 2 to 3 inches across. You can also harvest baby beets. The greens are delicious treated like chard or mustard greens, quickly sautéed. Leaf miners can be a nuisance to a beet crop, especially if you want to harvest the leaves. They leave large gray or brown patches on the greens where they have "mined" (tunneled through) the juicy green flesh of the plant's leaves. They are best controlled by hand picking the affected and unsightly leaves as soon as you notice any damage. Discard these leaves in a sealed plastic bag. Don't toss them on the compost pile because they will just take their own sweet time hatching and will return to your garden. Blue sticky traps are another good solution for trapping and halting the spread of the bugs.

VARIETIES **Bull's Blood** is the earliest of all the beet cultivars, maturing in just 35 to 50 days, and is somewhat resistant to leaf miners. **Detroit Dark Red** and **Early Wonder** (60 to 70 days) are reliable throughout the region and rich in flavor. The more delicately flavored and unusually colored **Golden Beet** (55 days) is very popular and is also fairly resistant to leaf miners. **Chioggia** (55 days) is the striking red-and-white striped beet; the stripes, however, tend to fade considerably when the beet is cooked.

Blackberries

Fat, shiny, black, sweet as summer, and juicy . . . the blackberry is a garden jewel to behold. We aren't talking about the roadside ramblers that will engulf your car should you venture into the ditch along a country road. These are the cultivated, select blackberries for the home garden, perfect for pies, tarts, and eating right off the cane or in a bowl with a fine dusting of sugar. Go ahead, mash a few of them and add some heavy cream. Can you smell summer?

GROWING Easy to grow, with a little foresight and preparation of their growing space, blackberries will give you a great return for your money. Choose thornless varieties, since they exist and so there is no reason to put up with berries that bite back.

Plant the canes away from the main vegetable garden, especially keeping them a good distance from any vegetables in the nightshade (Solanaceae) family: tomatoes, eggplants, potatoes, and peppers. Members of the nightshade family may carry diseases such as blight that are easily transmitted to the canes of blackberries, raspberries, and strawberries. They do very well in zones 5 to 9, withstanding cold temperatures to –10°F. Sadly, blackberries are not cold hardy enough for many parts of the intermountain region. But where they do thrive, they are a treat well worth growing. They produce best with full sun exposure and are self-pollinating. Most canes grow 4 to 6 feet tall, requiring a well-built trellis and annual pruning.

Purchase canes that are well developed, meaning sturdy, showing signs of new growth, and without bruises or blemishes. Plants start to produce when they are two years old and are fully mature when they are four to five years old, when they produce 5 to 6 pounds of fruit per cane per season. Well-planted blackberries are long lived, often producing for ten to fifteen years. Blackberries are especially well behaved if trained on a trellis.

Like other cane fruits, blackberries need a well-prepared planting site: soil that is amended with plenty of organic compost and has good drainage. They need regular deep, drip watering, preferably at the bottom of the cane, nearer the root system, instead of overhead watering; blackberry leaves like to stay dry, so they don't get fungal diseases. Water blackberry plants during the day and frequently the first two to three weeks after you plant them. Keep the top inch of soil moist. Apply water at the rate of 1 to 2 inches per week, or more if the weather is hot and dry.

HARVESTING Pick blackberries when the fruits are plump and evenly dark colored and any semblance of red fruit is gone. The berry should easily detach from the stem. You eat the entire berry; unlike the raspberry, it does not separate from the core. Ripe blackberries are fragile, so pick only a few layers of berries, then gently empty your container in a flat box before going back for more.

VARIETIES **Apache** is known for its jumbo, brightly flavored berries. It is ready to harvest very early for blackberries, in mid to late June. **Triple Crown** is famous for flavor, productivity, and vigor (though blackberries generally are known for their vigor). This variety ripens much later than Apache, often in late August or the first of September, and is a prolific producer of exceptionally large berries, excellent for pie, preserves, and syrups. **Black Satin** has erect canes and is heat tolerant, making it a good choice for the hot-summer parts of the Rockies; it bears in July.

Blueberries

Superfood, brainfood . . . just two nicknames for these wildly popular, deliciously sweet berries. And what a plant! Not only are the berries delicious to eat, but the blueberry shrub is beautiful to look at in the garden, so it is often placed among perennials as well as in the veggie garden. Clusters of dainty, waxy, bell-shaped, white flowers bloom in spring, becoming berries that are aromatic, dark blue, and frosted looking. The bushes have great ornamental value, with shiny bright green leaves turning to orange in fall and with attractive reddish brown stems in winter. Blueberry shrubs are perfect as part of informal plantings in native plant gardens or open woodlands.

GROWING Blueberries love organically rich, medium to wet, well-drained soil in full sun to part shade. In many parts of the intermountain west, afternoon shade is a must. The bush's shallow, fibrous roots need constant moisture and good drainage. Because our soils are very alkaline, and blueberries demand acidic soils, you may need to seriously amend the planting area with some granular sulfur. If amending the garden area is a difficult undertaking for you, blueberries do well when planted in large containers, where the acidity of the soil is easier to adjust.

Plants appreciate rich organic mulch. Prune as needed in late winter, beginning in the third year after planting. Blueberry bushes can be planted as close as 2 to 2½ feet apart to form solid hedgerows or spaced up to 6 feet apart and grown individually. When planting blueberry bushes, I recommend that you plant two bushes for each member of your family (so everyone gets a good share), and plant at least two different varieties for good cross pollination and fruit production: for instance, plant Blueray and Chandler together, or Blueray and Jersey.

A blueberry bush will be three to four years old before it will set fruit, but most of the bushes you buy at reputable nurseries are, in fact, mature enough to produce a few berries the first year they are planted. They can live to be twenty-five to fifty years old.

HARVESTING Blueberries are best tested for ripeness by tasting. They will be sweet and delicious. This is generally 2 or 3 days after they turn uniformly blue. They will also easily slip off the stem when they are ready to eat. Gently remove them from the plant and gather in a bowl or bucket.

VARIETIES The large delicious berries of **Early Blue** yield a moderate harvest at the end of June and into July. Plants are particularly intolerant of a wet growing site. The shrubs have a good red fall color. **Blueray**, which ripens in mid-July, performs particularly well in areas with hot summers and very cold winters, and produces high-quality, very large blueberries with outstanding dessert flavor. The stunning rosy pink flowers turn bright white when in full bloom. **Northland** ripens mid-June to mid-July and has small dark blue fruit with excellent wild berry flavor. This self-pollinating variety is the most cold hardy blueberry grown.

It has limber branches that do not break under heavy snow loads and it adapts well to subzero weather. **Chandler** is the world's largest blueberry. Its long ripening season starting in August will provide a bounty of fresh-picked fruit for over six weeks, when most varieties produce over just three to four weeks. **Hardyblue** is a very sweet, medium-sized berry with superior flavor. It is heavy yielding in midsummer and has appealing yellow fall color. Perhaps its best trait for our region is that it is especially tolerant of heavy clay soil. **Jersey** is a late-season bearer, the end of July and into August. It is one of the oldest, most widely grown varieties.

Broccoli

Yes, it's a member of the notoriously nutritious brassica family, and yes, it's very good for you. Broccoli is another cool-season crop that does well in our region. Broccoli rabe, or raab or rapini, is of Italian ancestry and considered a "sprouting" broccoli, which is characterized by many small shoots rather than a single head.

GROWING Start seeds indoors or purchase seedlings from a reputable nursery. Transplant new seedlings for best results. They may be purchased or sown inside weeks before the last frost. For a summer crop, plant when soil temperature reaches 60 to 70°F (early spring) and for a fall crop, plant seeds in shaded parts of the garden in mid-July. Space plants 18 inches apart, and amend the soil with a generous amount of alfalfa meal or pellets or some organic compost. Broccoli has shallow roots, so consistent, adequate water is a necessity. Tiny white butterflies (whitefly) may signal cabbage worms, notorious brassica pests. Don't ignore these: pick the worms off by hand or grow these crops under a row cover.

HARVESTING To harvest, broccoli heads should be firm and just starting to show a bit of looseness around the edges. Cut stems with a sharp knife and make the cut at an angle. Many varieties will produce a second crop of smaller heads. Broccoli rabe is a good cut-and-come-again example, growing quickly and prolifically in cool weather. You eat the shoots whole, including the leaves, stems, and buds.

VARIETIES Large-headed varieties include **Arcadia**, **Belstar**, and **Munchkin** (50 to 70 days for a spring crop; 65 to 90 days for an autumn crop). Sprouting types are **Calabrese**, **De Cicco**, and **Purple Sprouting** (same maturation rate as large head broccoli). Broccoli raab varieties that do well in our region are **Rapini** and **Sorrento** (65 to 70 days). All broccoli has a pronounced sweetness when harvested in cool autumn weather.

Brussels Sprouts

A tasty cool-weather vegetable, member of the renowned nutritious brassica family, Brussels sprouts are easily grown in the home garden. Especially well suited for high altitude, short-season gardens, they ask only three things of you: adequate water, full sun, and some space. Brussels sprouts were so named since they were a favorite Belgian vegetable. The first written record of them is from 1587, and they were grown near the city of Brussels, possibly since the 1300s.

GROWING Seeds for Brussels sprout plants can be planted in a protected area or grown in a greenhouse in trays. The seeds should be planted ¼ inch deep and covered with fine soil. When the seedlings are 4 inches tall and four weeks old, they are ready to go in the garden. Brussels sprouts grow best where the air temperature ranges between 45 and 75°F. They don't do well if temperatures are too hot or too cold.

The other option is to purchase seedlings. When transplanting either, take care not to disturb the finicky roots. Brussels sprouts appreciate a nitrogen-rich soil, one that has been amended by adding a 3-inch layer of composted leaves or a 2-inch top dressing of alfalfa, soybean, or cottonseed meal. Transplants should be placed in the garden at the same depth as they were growing as seedlings. Handle transplants with care, trying not to disturb the roots. Members of the brassica family—cabbage, broccoli, kale, Brussels sprouts—do not tolerate drought. They are happiest with even, deep watering and a 2- to 3-inch layer of mulch to retain that moisture and keep the roots cool.

HARVESTING Brussels sprouts tend to sweeten in flavor if they've stood through a couple of light frosts. When the sprouts look like tiny 1-inch cabbages, you can start harvesting them from the bottom of the plant stalk. Cut them off cleanly with a sharp knife. The sprouts mature from the bottom up, so as the season progresses, you will work your way up the stem.

VARIETIES **Long Island Improved** (80 to 150 days) is an old-time favorite, prolific at producing those tasty little buds over an extended period. **Falstaff** (98 days) is a prized purple-red variety, new to most gardeners but all the rage in gourmet restaurants. They even retain some of their color when cooked. **Jade Cross**, a hybrid, has been around for at least fifty years and is still an all-time favorite because it is highly productive, vigorous, and takes only 80 days or so to mature.

Cabbage

Cabbage can be seeded directly into the garden in early spring, or set out as transplants. In the coldest areas, transplants are recommended. A combination of crinkly and colored varieties will add visual interest to your edible garden or perennial border.

GROWING Cabbage plants are shallow rooted and love rich garden soil: fertile, moist, well-drained, and full of organic matter. Plant them 24 inches apart in each direction. Seeds should be planted ¼ to ½ inch deep. Especially heavy feeders, cabbages and other cole crops love soils that have been amended heavily with organic composted manure.

HARVESTING Cabbage can be harvested anytime after the heads form, preferably before they split. Heads should be firm and well formed. Remove the head from the plant by cutting it off the stem, close to the head. If you discover a split cabbage, harvest and use as soon as possible.

VARIETIES **Early Jersey Wakefield** (60 to 85 days), developed in England in 1840, has conical heads, and is good for small gardens. **Danish Ballhead** (85 to 110 days), from Denmark in the fifteenth century, is slow to bolt or split, and grows well in cooler areas. **Perfection Drumhead Savoy** (95 days) has crinkled leaves and is a good keeper.

TIP *The "cole" crops—broccoli, Brussels sprouts, cabbage, cauliflower, kale, and kohlrabi—also known as crops in the brassica family, have similar growing requirements and pest issues. (A cole crop is not to be confused with "cold." Cole, in Latin, means stem or cabbage.) Beware of cabbage worms and their parents, white cabbage butterflies, or whitefly. They can be controlled organically by removing the caterpillars when you see them or spraying the plants with Bt, or* Bacillus thuringiensis *(see page 33). A floating row cover over newly planted transplants or newly sown beds will be very helpful. Flea beetles and aphids can be knocked off the plants with a strong spray of cold water.*

Cantaloupe, Muskmelon, Honeydew Melon, and Watermelon

Cool and delicious, any of the melons—cantaloupes, muskmelons, honeydews, and watermelons—are a quintessential summer vegetable garden treat. Scientists divide melons into just two types, watermelons and melons. Our beloved cantaloupe, with its tan skin and corky, netlike pattern, is actually a muskmelon. True cantaloupes are rarely grown in the United States. But we'll use the terms cantaloupe and muskmelon interchangeably, like most folks in the States do. Honeydews have a luscious pale green flesh, very sweet flavor, and a pale yellow-green smooth rind. Watermelons now range in size from the very small "personal or individual" melons to the jumbo, old-fashioned, striped or dotted green beauties. Other than making watermelon rind pickles, there is little you can do to preserve melons, so grow them with care and relish every fresh, juicy bite.

Gardeners in the higher elevations of our region will need to employ various strategies to successfully grow watermelons and cantaloupes, while folks in the warmer regions will be easily successful. In the intermountain west, famous melon-growing regions are Hermiston, Oregon, Green River, Utah, and Rocky Ford, Colorado.

GROWING Wait for the soil to warm up to before planting any of the melons. Soil temperatures should be good and warm—65°F—before you transplant melon seedlings or direct sow them in the garden. A layer of black plastic will help warm up the soil and keep weeds at bay in the melon patch. Create hills or mounds, about 12 inches across and 4 feet apart in each direction. Plant the seeds 1 to 2 inches deep, and water thoroughly. When the first set of leaves appears, thin to one strong plant per hill. Hot caps may be needed to protect these tender plants until the weather is reliably warm. Melons also do well when put in the garden as transplants. To prevent cutworms and their damage, you can put a paper collar around the newly sprouted seedlings or transplants. Make the paper collar about 2 inches tall and at least 3 inches in diameter. Drip irrigation is highly recommended for melons. If cucumber beetles or squash borers are a problem, remove them by hand. Choose varieties resistant to Fusarium wilt.

HARVESTING Cantaloupes and muskmelons are ready when the color changes from green to pale tan and the melon stem slips easily from the vine, which is called "full slip." Honeydew melons are ripe when they turn slightly golden and are fragrant. Watermelons have a "ground spot" on the rind where the fruit was in contact with the ground; it will turn from white to yellow when the fruit is ready to harvest.

VARIETIES Seeds for heirloom varieties are becoming easier to find, since the demand for these tasty heritage fruits has skyrocketed. If you want a particularly rare variety, order seeds early from one of the purveyors mentioned in Resources at the back of the book. Some melon varieties originated more than 100 years ago. **Rocky Ford Green Flesh** (85 days), a juicy, green muskmelon, 1 to 2 pounds, is a great keeper. **Jenny Lind** (80 days) is a lime-green, turban-shaped muskmelon. **Minnesota Midget**, an excellent choice for the cooler areas of our region, is a very small, incredibly sweet muskmelon that matures in as little as 75 to 90 days. The vines are just 4 feet long. The incredibly tasty **Afghan Honeydew** melon (90 days) is only 8 inches long and shaped like a football. **Klondike Blue Ribbon Striped** (90 days) is a heavy, sweet heirloom watermelon. **Moon and Stars** watermelon (100 days) was named for the gorgeous pattern on the skin.

Carrots

Carrots are one of those glorious jewel-colored vegetables considered good for you. They are full of beta-carotene and lycopene, eaten by pilots to improve their vision, a valuable source of fiber, and a staple of every veggie tray, lunch box, and salad bar in America. Surprisingly enough, carrots can be yellow, white, red, or dark purple. In fact, the original carrots were purple and white.

GROWING The beauty of root crops is that they are easily grown from seed, they don't need transplanting (in fact, they resent it), and they adore cool weather, which makes them perfect for the higher, cooler regions of the Rockies. They do love a soft, loose soil: one that will allow them to grow straight and strong. Carefully chose a variety well suited to your particular growing region. Nantes varieties come on fast and mature quickly, so they are a good choice for early crops, before it gets hot. By sowing a variety that needs more time to mature, you can stretch the harvest into fall (and in many cases you can overwinter them in the ground).

Two weeks before your last frost date, sow your carrots. They need warm soil, 60 to 70°F, to develop. Sow carrots in well-worked soil, mixing the carrot seeds half and half with radish seeds. This is called using a "nurse crop," which is a crop that provides shelter and protection from weeds, aiding in the success of the main crop. The radishes develop quickly, and when you harvest them, they leave space for the carrots to develop. Keep the soil moist— not soaking wet—the first 10 days after sowing to aid in germination. Even more helpful, put a layer of clean grass clippings right on top of the area that was seeded. The grass clippings are lightweight but keep the newly sown area moist. Drip irrigation is a benefit to carrot seeds, since it effectively delivers water only to the carrot root zone. Soak deeply. You can sow additional carrot crops every two to three weeks, ensuring a long harvest period.

Carrot rust fly can be an issue, but not in all parts of our region. It may be a problem on one end of a valley and not the other. Row covers will deter them.

HARVESTING To make harvesting easier, use a garden fork or pitchfork to loosen the soil around the carrots before you harvest them.

VARIETIES **Nantes** (62 days) types, which originated in or near the town of Nantes, France, are the most widely grown of all carrots. Good choices for sowing early include **Scarlet Nantes** (68 days), **Bolero** (75 days), **Nelson** (58 days), **Touchon** (65 days), **Yaya** (60 days), and **White Satin** (70 days). Other varieties are **Chantenay** (65 days), **Danvers Half Long** (75 days), **Purple Haze** (73 days), **Dragon** (85 days, dark purple), and **Napoli** (58 days). When sliced, Purple Haze displays a striking yellow and orange core. **Yellowstone** (70 days) has a rich yellow color, the sweet carrot flavor is improved when roasted or cooked, and it holds well in the winter garden. **Tonda Di Parigi** (60 days) is the cute little orange ball carrot, especially good for shallow growing spaces. While this carrot has an Italian sounding name, it is famous in France, and originated (as did most carrots) in Afghanistan.

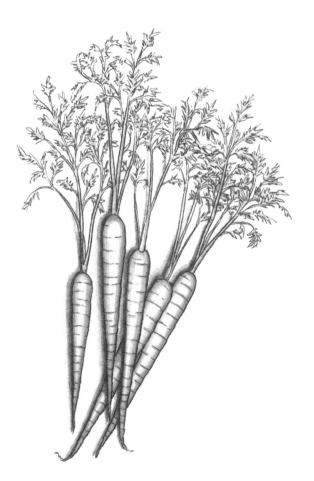

Cauliflower

The beautiful white, yellow, green, or purple crowns (heads) of cauliflower are especially mild in flavor if grown with plenty of moisture and attention. Cauliflower does best growing in the cooler parts of our region. In the hotter areas, like Boise, Reno, or Salt Lake, you will want to grow it as an autumn crop.

GROWING Set out spring transplants early enough so that they can mature before the heat of summer but not so early that they might freeze; two to four weeks before the last frost is about right. Be prepared to protect them from cold weather with a cover. Set out fall crops about six to eight weeks before the first frost. Be prepared to shade them, if needed, to protect from heat. Position each plant at least 24 inches from its nearest neighbor. Water thoroughly and regularly. The soil should be kept moist but not waterlogged at least 6 inches below the surface. If allowed to dry out too often, the heads will "rice," or fall apart, and become bitter. Protect the roots with a 1- to 2-inch layer of mulch.

Beware of cabbage worms—sometimes called "loopers" because of the way they move along the plant, like an inchworm—and their parents, white cabbage butterflies, or whitefly. If you see small, white butterflies around the garden, look closely for the larvae on the back side of the plant leaves. The caterpillars are 1 to 2 inches long, green, sometimes with silver or white stripes. In a green garden, they can be hard to find. They can be controlled organically by removing the caterpillars when you see them or spraying the plants with Bt. A floating row cover over newly planted transplants or newly sown beds will be very helpful. Flea beetles and aphids can be knocked off the plants with a strong spray of cold water.

When the cauliflower heads are almost full size, pull the leaves up and around the heads to blanche them, or keep them white. You can use a bamboo skewer to sew the leaves together. Leave the purple-headed varieties uncovered. Cauliflower can withstand light frosts.

Another cauliflower type, Romanesco, or Roman cauliflower, is worth finding, for its striking appearance, with spiral, pointy projections and lime-green color. Space plants about 18 inches apart.

HARVESTING When the head is between 6 and 12 inches in diameter, and the tiny flowers are still closed, cut the head from the stem with a sharp knife.

VARIETIES **Early Snowball** (60 days) is a good choice for both spring or fall planting. **LeCerf** (75 days) has large heads and big leaves that aid in the blanching process. **Violetta Italia** (85 days) is a purple-headed variety that turns creamy white when cooked. **Veronica** (78 days) is a good Romanesco variety.

Chard

Swiss chard has deeply colored green leaves, all crinkly and shiny, and stems that are red, white, school bus yellow, or sometimes all three! With all these glowing attributes, it is also very nutritious, especially when served just moments after harvesting. Chard has become the darling edible of the ornamental gardening world. Add it to containers of summer annuals.

GROWING Plant seeds directly into the soil, ½-inch deep, 8 inches apart, two weeks before the last frost, and again ten weeks before the first frost for a fall crop. Chard likes cool, damp soil, so a 3-inch layer of mulch will aid in keeping the roots cool and moist.

HARVESTING When the leaves appear, and are 4 to 6 inches high, harvest the leaves as baby greens. In two to three weeks, the leaves will be 6 to 10 inches long, and at maturity, about 18 inches. If growing in a row, thin the leaves and plants as they develop, with a goal of 18 to 24 inches between plants. Since chard seeds are actually capsules containing more than a single seed, use small scissors to remove any leaves crowding the strongest stem.

VARIETIES Swiss chard comes in a colorful blend called **Bright Lights** (35 days for young leaves, 60 days for mature), **Rainbow Chard** (35 to 60 days), as well as a beautiful red-veined cultivar, **Ruby Red Rhubarb** chard (32 days for baby leaves, 59 days for full size), whose pretty red stalks are sometimes pickled. **Fordhook Giant** (50 to 60 days), the classic, old-fashioned variety, has white stems, excellent productivity, and is slow to bolt, with great flavor. A cousin called **Perpetual Spinach Chard** (50 to 60 days) looks like spinach but tastes like chard. It produces for a long time, and the more you pick, the more it grows.

Corn

Originally from semitropical climates, corn is a historic traditional crop, providing sustenance for native peoples and animals alike. Corn, or maize, has been in cultivation as a food crop for thousands of years. Originally from Mexico and as far south as Costa Rica, explorers and traders carried and introduced maize to Europe. In the form of grain or cornmeal, it is a staple food and the main ingredient of tortillas, tamales, tacos, enchiladas, and many other Mexican dishes. Summer isn't summer until you've had your first ear of fresh corn on the cob—preferably just minutes off the stalk, briefly broiled or grilled, and dripping with butter. Heirloom varieties are prized for their short-season adaptation as well as their colorful kernels.

GROWING Corn should not be sown until the soil temperature is at least 50°F. Plant corn every two weeks or plant both early and late-season varieties to get an extended harvest. Plant corn on the north side of your garden, in rows within blocks at least 4 by 6 feet to ensure adequate wind-pollination among the plants. For early plantings, sow seeds only 1 inch deep; if the temperatures have gotten very hot, plant them up to 2 inches deep. Thin to 1 plant every 15 inches, and remove unwanted seedlings by cutting them off at soil level. Corn does take up a lot of space, but it's easy to grow and so yummy when just picked. And it is a very interesting plant, with little toes around the bottom of the stalk to keep it upright.

HARVESTING Keep an eye on the corn as the ears develop, and watch the silk (the tassels sprouting out of the top of each husk) as it turns colors and changes texture. When it dries up, the ear is almost ready to harvest. Carefully pull back the husk and push your fingernail into a kernel, and if it spouts a milky substance, it is ready to pick.

VARIETIES **Country Gentleman** (Shoepeg) (88 to 100 days) is a white corn with nonrowed kernels. **Stowell's Evergreen** (80 to 100 days), is a leading white heirloom cultivar. If you can find this old variety, it is worth growing. **Golden Bantam** (70 to 85 days) was one of the first yellow sweet corns for human use and the "gold" standard for home gardeners. It is open-pollinated (OP), or pollinated by the mechanisms of nature, like birds, insects, or wind.

Cucumbers

The fresh, cool crispness of homegrown cucumbers is another summer pleasure for vegetable gardeners. Fresh from the vine, they surpass any hot-house or store-bought version. Their fresh, mild taste makes them a favorite salad ingredient, and they are especially welcome on the dinner table in the high heat of summer.

GROWING One of the hotties, cucumbers crave warm weather. The seeds and plants do not want to be in the ground until it has warmed up considerably. You can start plants from seeds indoors, four to six weeks before all danger of frost has passed, or you can successfully—and almost as quickly—grow them from seed sown directly in the garden at that time.

Plant them in hills, making the hills 36 to 48 inches apart where the vines can sprawl, or train the vines up a trellis. Create a mound of soil by pushing it together and up 4 inches high and 12 inches across. Tamp it down slightly on the top and sides to hold its shape. Poke three seeds in each mound, 1 inch deep and 6 inches apart. Water the planted seeds gently but well. When the plants are up and have developed a second set of leaves, thin to 12 inches apart, often leaving just one plant—the strongest one—per hill to allow it to thrive and spread out.

HARVESTING It is important to harvest cucumbers while they are young. As cucumbers get bigger, the seeds inside get larger and less edible, and the vine will stop producing new fruits.

For slicing varieties, pick them before they are 6 inches long; for pickling types, pick them at 3 inches.

VARIETIES **Lemon** (58 to 70 days) is an oval, yellow slicer. The **Armenian** cucumber (50 to 75 days), also known as snake melon, is not really a cucumber but a member of the melon family. But it tastes just like a cucumber and is delicious and amazingly crisp. **Japanese Climbing** (58 to 65 days) is a perfect slicer for growing on trellises or fences and in small spaces. **Straight 8** (52 to 75 days) is an All-American Selection that bears 8-inch-long fruits.

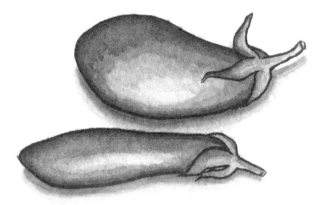

Eggplant

Often described as odd or interesting, eggplant is a traditional food in Old World countries. You can grow them in our region if you live in an area with a long, warm growing season. They are delicious grilled, sautéed, stir-fried, or baked with tomatoes and cheese in renowned dishes such as eggplant parmesan or moussaka.

GROWING Eggplant plants need to be kept warm and protected. You can find standard types as seedlings, and some of the more exotic varieties can only be found as seeds. If you are starting them from seed, sow indoors at least eight weeks before the last frost. This will allow the plants to develop strong stems and root systems. Keep them warm and well watered but not soggy. Do not be fooled into buying eggplant starts early. They often appear in the garden centers way before it is warm enough to plant them outdoors. Set them out into the garden when the ambient air temperature is 70°F during the day and all danger of frost is passed. You may need to use hot caps or cloches if night temperatures are still cool. If you

position the plants near a warm wall, that will be a big help. Eggplants need a deep drink of water once or twice a week.

HARVESTING Eggplant is best harvested when the skin is still shiny. When the luster fades from the skin, the seeds have started to develop and may impart a bitter taste to the fruit. It's best to use a sharp pair of pruners or kitchen shears to cut the eggplant from the stem, leaving 1 inch of stem on the fruit.

VARIETIES **Ichiban** and **Ping Tung Long** (both 70 days), Asian types, are widely available in transplant form, and bear fruits that are long and narrow—12 to 18 inches long and 2 inches wide. **Black Beauty** (80 days) is a large, beautiful purple eggplant. **Kermit** (60 days), a wonder to behold, produces charming small 3- to 4-inch-long fruits. **Turkish Orange** (75 days) is an heirloom variety. **Rosa Bianca** (83 days), another heirloom, has fruits that are 6 inches long. **Listada de Gandia** (80 days) is an eye catching and very tasty Spanish cultivar with 7-inch-long fruits.

Garlic

Garlic enjoys a vivid reputation not only as a health food, but also as a flavorful cooking ingredient. Varieties of hard-neck garlic, with their delicious spring scapes, are best suited to our region, coping well with our soils, cooler temperatures, and arid climates.

Elephant garlic isn't really garlic at all, but a shirttail cousin and member of the leek family. The wow factor of elephant garlic comes from several attributes: the plant often grows 4 to 5 feet tall. As befitting such a statuesque plant, it develops a softball-size bulb with a mild mannered, mellow garlic flavor.

GROWING Most garlic is planted in the fall and harvested from early summer until early fall. Be sure to use only state-certified garlic bulbs for planting (see page 220). Garlic is very easy to plant: just crack the bulb by breaking off each clove, one at a time, from the basal plate (the flat area at the bottom of the bulb) where the cloves come together and the roots grow. Within 24 hours, plant each single clove, 1 inch deep, 4 to 6 inches apart, in rich, loamy soil amended with organic compost. Be sure to plant with the pointy end up (the flat end you broke away is the bottom and where the new roots will develop). In the coldest regions of the intermountain west, provide a thick winter mulch of 4 inches of leaves.

Elephant garlic should be given more room to grow. So plant cloves 6 to 8 inches apart and top with 4 to 6 inches of soil. Plant in October or November. Water in the spring when fresh green growth appears, but reduce water a couple weeks prior to harvest (late summer).

HARVESTING When ready to harvest, carefully dig up each multi-cloved bulb, remove excess soil, and hang loosely in clumps of four to six bulbs, in a dry, cool, dark place for two weeks. Make sure the garlic has good air circulation between bulbs.

VARIETIES Good reliable, productive varieties for our region are **Chesnok Red** and **Persian Star** (90 to 150 days). **Elephant Garlic** just goes by that name, elephant garlic.

Herbs

Herbs are widely diverse group of plants used in myriad applications, including medicine, fragrances, cooking, and insect repellents. They are used in religious ceremonies and floral bouquets, and they are wildly attractive as well as beneficial to birds, bees, butterflies, and other pollinators, offering food and shelter to their offspring. Their natural history, which goes back thousands of years, is the subject of countless books. Here, I can only deal with the tip of the herbal iceberg. Herbs play an important role in our lives, with their medicinal values, spiritual associations, and ability to season foods. Rosemary is one of the most famous herbs, a valued symbol of friendship. Herbs, such as parsley, thyme, savory, and basil, not only cleanse the palate, but add another dimension to what might otherwise be a ho-hum dish. You may find it fascinating to study herbs in depth, if you get a chance.

GROWING As a general rule, herbs like lean soil, lots of sun, and prefer to be on the dry side, which makes most of them excellent candidates for our Rocky Mountain region and its lean, dry soils. The exception is basil, which loves plenty of water. Basil is one of few herbs needing to be seeded each year; most herbs tend to be perennial, tender perennials, or self-seeding. Herb gardens should not be fertilized, since a soil that is too rich causes weak growth in the plant and lackluster essence and oils. An occasional soil drench of comfrey tea and an annual top dressing of organic compost are the only feedings your herbs will need.

When planting purchased perennial herbs, carefully remove them from the pot they were growing in, and place them in a same-sized hole and at the same level in the soil as they were in the pot. Herbs like well-drained soil and can't abide standing water. If planting them in a container, use a good organic potting soil. If making your own potting mix, use 7 parts good soil, 3 parts fine bark or compost, and 2 parts coarse sand. If planting in the ground, add a handful of fine bark or compost to the soil mix you will be backfilling with. This improves tilth and drainage, and will slowly feed the existing soil.

Stem cuttings are an economical and easy way to increase the number of herb plants you have. Use this procedure:

- Choose a healthy plant to take cuttings from.
- Take short cuttings about 3 to 4 inches long from new growth on the branch.
- Carefully remove the leaves from the bottom part of the cutting, which will be inserted in the soil, leaving only a few small leaves at the top.
- Place your cuttings in a container filled with soil-free planting medium, only 2 to 3 inches deep.
- Water in.

If planting rooted cuttings, create a new hole for the plant, place the cutting in the hole, and backfill with soil, leaving the leafy part above the soil line. Gently pat the soil in place and water gently.

In the spring, give perennial overwintered herbs a good haircut and nice drink of water. Remove all the debris from around the base of the plant. Keep weeds away from the plants, judiciously mulching around them. Most perennial herbs can take a slight frost, but basil cannot. One degree too cold and basil becomes a slimy black mess.

SPECIES AND VARIETIES Of the numerous kinds of herbs grown in the garden, the following are some of the most popular:

Basil is one herb you must grow in the garden. Store-bought weaklings cannot compare to homegrown plants, since the leaves need proper sun and air to develop their pungent flavor. There are as few as 50 and maybe as many as 150 varieties of basil, in a kaleidoscope of colors, including **Holy**, **Cinnamon**, **Spicy Globe**, **Thai**, **African Blue**, **Purple**, **Lemon**, and **Lime**. **Sweet** basil or **Genovese** basil is a requirement for a proper tomato salad dressed simply with a little olive oil, balsamic vinegar, and salt and pepper.

Start basil seeds directly in the garden, after all danger of frost has past and when the nighttime temps are above 55°F. To get a jump on the season, grow your own basil seedlings in the house or in a cold frame until it is time to set them out in the garden. You can start cutting leaves when the plant reaches 6 to 8 inches in height. And keep pinching the plant back to encourage it to keep producing.

Chives and garlic chives are herbaceous perennial herbs. They tend to die back in winter. The globe-shaped, lavender blossoms of chives are used for garnishing dishes, and the stems and leaves are good torn into salads and chopped for sprinkling over other dishes. For a quick start, ask a gardening friend for a clump of chives and transplant them into your garden. You can plant seeds, but they may take up a year to be of a harvestable size. To harvest, snip with scissors. Garlic chives have flattened wider leaves, larger heads of white flowers, and a subtle garlic flavor. They have several aliases: Chinese chives, oriental garlic, and Chinese leek. **Fine Leaf** (75 to 85 days) chives variety is delicate and very mild. **Staro** (75 to 85 days) is a bit sturdier and holds up well for freezing and drying.

Cilantro (60 to 90 days) is a pungent annual herb used extensively in Mexican and Asian cuisine. Cilantro is the foliage and coriander is the seed of the plant. Look for a variety called **Slow Bolt**, which holds up well in hotter areas.

Dill is an annual herb, but quite often it will sow itself around the garden. In biblical times, dill was so prized it could be used to pay your taxes. Still very valuable for making dill pickles and as an accompaniment to salmon dishes, it is a great host plant for beneficial insects. Both the leaves and seeds are used; the seeds have a stronger taste, the leaves a more delicate taste. It's best to direct sow the seeds in the garden mid spring. **Dukat** is a favorite variety (40 to 60 days).

Fennel is another herb that can be used in its entirety. The fine foliage, when snipped, adds a distinctive anise or licorice flavor to a green salad (40 to 60 days). The dried seeds are widely used in Indian cuisine. The bulb (base) of **Florence** fennel is used as a vegetable, either raw or cooked. A member of the umbellifer family (with umbrella-shaped flowers), like dill, it is loved by pollinators. Considered a hardy perennial, fennel is easily grown from seed and eagerly sows itself around. A determined taproot makes a seedling very difficult to transplant.

Horseradish (180 days) is extremely pungent. A large, invasive, tough plant, it is best planted in a container or at the edge of the garden. Cuttings, divisions, or new plants can be purchased or begged from a friend, and should be planted 2 inches deep. Water in well. When planted in a rich soil with some afternoon shade, it will grow well with little care. The fresh roots can be dug spring to fall. The later they are harvested, the stronger the flavor. It's advisable to grate horseradish out of doors.

Lavender has a remarkable fragrance, and the plant has countless uses. Lavender is edible, but a little goes a long way. Use it to scent sugar or for making teas. **Munstead** is the hardiest (to zone 4); it and **Hidcote** are considered the best varieties for culinary use. Lavender plants need to be carefully sited in the garden, where they will get excellent drainage, and in the coldest areas, they like a warm microclimate against a south-facing wall or rock. Since lavender does not always come true from seed, purchase small transplants in the early spring, or obtain soft tissue cuttings from a friend. If your soil is not sandy, add a handful of sand or fine gravel to the planting hole. Water in well, but be stingy with water once the plant has become established (90 to 180 days to maturity).

Marjoram (sweet), and **Oregano**. Most folks can't tell marjoram (*Origanum majorana*), an annual, from its cousin, the perennial oregano (*O. vulgare*). Both have a distinctive heady, spicy fragrance, and no kitchen should be without at least one. Used extensively in tomato, pasta, and meat dishes, its botanical name means "joy of the mountain." One small plant can be divided into two and planted in full sun with very good drainage. By keeping the plant

lightly trimmed and not letting it flower, you encourage it to create new growth and strengthen it for overwintering. **Greek** and the **Hot and Spicy** cultivars have the most intense flavor, fresh or dried. **Italian** and **Santa Cruz** are much milder (all are 80 to 90 days).

Mint comes in many flavors: apple mint, chocolate mint, orange, peppermint, pineapple mint, and spearmint. A garden dominator, mint is best grown in a pot, sitting on a rock, where the roots cannot sneak out the drainage hole and across town. But mint is also a delicious, fragrant, refreshing herb that can be grown from seed or divisions. It is versatile and aromatic, repels ants, freshens closets and your breath, makes a fine tea, and is a zesty addition to a salad. Grow it anywhere (60 days from seed).

Parsley has moved beyond its ubiquitous place as an attractive garnish on your restaurant plate. **Curly** parsley is tightly curled, full of flavor, and is a tasty addition to a green salad. Its cousin, **Italian** or flat-leaf parsley (70 to 90 days) is favored by cooks and is a bit stronger in flavor. Both love afternoon shade, rich, well-tilled soil, and good drainage. Sow seeds in a prepared area when the air temperatures are reliably above 50°F at night. They may take two to four weeks to germinate. Let a few seeds re-sow for a crop the following season.

Rosemary, the herb of remembrance, is intensely flavored. Both the flowers and the leaves can be used in cooking. Provide rosemary with excellent drainage, a sheltered microclimate with a southern exposure, and, during the coldest winters, protect it with a wrap of horticultural fleece, if necessary. A tender perennial, you may want to bring your plant in if you live in zones 3 to 5. Water sparingly. Rosemary is easily propagated by stem cuttings. Cut a 5-inch branch, remove the lower 2 inches of leaves, and put the naked stem in a glass of water. When fine white roots appear, the stem can be planted into the garden, leaving the top 3 inches with leaves above the soil line. **Arp** is the hardiest of all the varieties (85 days). Any rosemary labeled *Rosmarinus officinalis* is edible.

Sage has many plant types(85 to 90 days). It is a graceful addition to the perennial border because of its attractive foliage, and it is fabulous in the kitchen for its flavor and aroma. Sage loves full sun, good drainage, and a modest amount of water. It can be sown directly in the garden in late spring when the evening temperatures are consistently above 45°F. You can also make cuttings (as described for Rosemary). **Berggarten**'s large leaves rarely blooms, extending their useful life. **Garden Sage** is the most commonly found cultivar. **Tricolor** has pretty white, yellow, and green variegated leaves. **Purple** is prized for its rich purple leaves.

Savory comes in both an annual (summer) form and perennial (overwintering) form. Winter savory is a hardy, shrubby evergreen with spicy, peppery aromatic leaves. By keeping it pruned and shaped, and occasionally pruning it all the way to the ground, you will be encouraging lots of new growth. Winter savory can be propagated by taking stem cuttings, and summer savory can be seeded.

Tarragon is considered an aristocratic herb, and has a subtle, spicy, anise-y flavor. It is an essential ingredient in the Fines Herbes and Bouquet Garni mixes. Be sure to purchase true French tarragon; it should be labeled Artemesia dracunculus (90 days). An imposter, A. dracunculoides, is slightly bitter. Tarragon is best purchased from a reliable nursery or propagated by root cuttings. Cut back to the ground every spring, and keep it shaped and lightly pruned throughout the growing season to encourage fresh new leaves.

Thyme comes in many varieties, so be sure you are getting a true culinary variety. **English** thyme, **Garden** thyme, **Golden** thyme, and **Lemon** thyme (90 days) are all excellent choices for the herb garden. Thyme loves full sun and gets by with very little water. Do give it a couple of good haircuts throughout the growing season to encourage fresh leaves. Thyme can be grown from seed, but it's more reliable to purchase a couple of nice plants and divide them up for the garden. Remove the plant from the container, and using a very sharp knife, cut straight through the plant from top to bottom. Replant in the garden at the same depth they were in the pot. Water in gently. Thyme loves good drainage.

Kale, Collards, and Mustard Greens

Packing a one-two knockout nutritional punch, kale, collards, and mustard greens can be squeezed in anywhere you have an extra foot of space, including and especially in the ornamental border and flower containers. Kale can be grown in a loose head similar to cabbage, or you can grow the distinctive silver-green Dinosaur kale, with its blistery, bumpy leaves. Collards grow in very loose heads with green-blue leaves that have a frosted cast to them. If you can, try to grow a very cool-season or winter crop of these dark green vegetables. They develop an especially bright, invigorating flavor in cool weather. Mustard greens are spicy on the tongue and beautifully ornamental in the garden.

GROWING These greens are best grown by planting seeds directly into the garden soil, ¼ to ½ inch deep, 6 to 12 inches apart. When they are up a few inches, generally in 25 days, you can harvest the leaves as baby greens. If growing in a row, thin and eat the thinnings as you go, ultimately creating a space between plants of 18 inches to 30 inches. Collards hold up better in hot weather, making them a hearty green for gardens in southwestern Idaho, Utah, and Nevada. Mustards are generally heat tolerant and can take light frosts as well.

HARVESTING Kale, collards, and mustard greens can be harvested from the outside in as the leaves develop. Or you can cut an entire clump of the leaves, clean off at the base. These plants are so resilient, they may sprout a few new leaves for you.

VARIETIES Kale is beloved by gourmet restaurants and foodies alike, the favorite being **Nero di Toscana** (50 days), which goes by many aliases such as Tuscan kale, cavolo nero, palm tree kale, black Tuscan palm, and Dinosaur kale. Another good cultivar is **Red Russian** (50 to 60 days), also known as **Ragged Jack**, courtesy of Russian traders more than a century ago. **Georgian Southern** collards (65 to 80 days) perform well in warmer parts of the Rockies. **Japanese Giant Red** mustard (45 days) is strongly flavored, excellent in stir-fries or pickled. **Garnet Giant** and **Ruby Streaks** make wonderful additions to container plantings (can be harvested in 20 days for small greens, 45 days for mature leaves).

Kohlrabi

Kohlrabi is one of the oddest looking vegetables ever grown, with multiple leaf stems growing out from around the swollen underground stem. The purple varieties are often used in ornamental plantings. The swollen stem of the kohlrabi is prized, and the leaves can be steamed or eaten fresh. The purple variety is so eye catching you can grow it in your flowerpots. Kohlrabi has a very mild cabbage- or turnip-like flavor and lends itself well to oven roasting with olive oil, salt, and pepper, or included into a root vegetable gratin. Kohlrabi is a member of the cabbage (brassica) family, so keep that in mind when planning your crop rotation.

GROWING Kohlrabi can be direct sown three weeks before the last frost or started indoors six weeks before the last frost. Transplant the seedlings into the garden one month later. Thin kohlrabi to 12 inches apart in all directions. They need plenty of even moisture, so don't let them dry out, or the result will be a bitter, pithy, inedible root. Rows should be 18 inches apart. Handpick cabbage worms or apply a dusting of Bt.

HARVESTING The bulb will be sitting above the ground when it's ready to harvest. Just pull the plant from the soil or cut it off cleanly at the soil level. If necessary, use a spading fork. Harvest purple kohlrabi when the stems are just 3 inches in diameter.

VARIETIES **Early White Vienna** (55 days) and **Sweet Vienna** (45 days) have pale creamy flesh and are garden favorites. **Purple Vienna** (60 days) is a gorgeous thing, pale lavender with a light green interior.

Leeks and Bunching Onions

This category of onions grows straight and tall, has green shanks, and will not produce a bulb. The group goes by several names: scallions, Welsh onions, green onions, and spring onions. Leeks are the tall, strong, husky cousins of the green onion. Bunching onions are essentially a scallion (green onion) type. Generally, only the white portion of the leek is used, for hearty soups, and sometimes, cut in half and grilled or sautéed. They can also be used raw, in salads, since they have a mild onion flavor. The entire portion, green and white, of smaller scallions can be used in fresh salads and stir-fries.

GROWING Leeks are best grown to be eaten when you use the process known as "blanching." You keep pulling the soil up around the stem as the leek grows to protect it from sunlight, so that the root end remains white and tender. Leeks can be started from seed and transplanted as seedlings into the garden. Or you can sow seeds directly into the garden. Choose a part of the garden where you can make a trench to sow them and later mound the soil

for the blanching process. Sow the seed sparsely on top of well-worked, finely raked soil. Sprinkle a light layer of soil on top of the seeds, only ⅛ to ¼ inch deep. When the wispy seedlings are up, start gently pulling the soil up around each plant to the line where the green stem begins. As the seedlings grow, add more soil to protect the white part of the leek from the sunlight. Bunching onions don't need to be blanched. Both plants, along with all other members of the onion family, need at least 1 inch of water per week.

HARVESTING Leeks are ready when they are 1 inch in diameter. Harvest bunching onions when they are just ⅓ inch in diameter.

VARIETIES **King Richard**, **Large American Flag**, **Titan**, and **Giant Musselburgh** are excellent disease-resistant leek cultivars. Leeks need 120 to 150 days to mature, but newer varieties are becoming available that might be ready in 90 days. For bunching onions, the **Evergreen Hardy Bunching** (65 days) will survive temperatures as low as −25°F. **Long White** and **Red Baron** will be ready in 60 days.

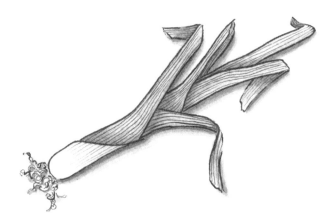

Lettuce

Oh, how far we've come from the plain old iceberg lettuce salad with a dollop of Thousand Island dressing on it. You can now easily grow a colorful variety of tasty lettuce leaves for your salad bowl. There are so many types of lettuce, in fact, that it's hard to know what to choose.

Lettuce is categorized in groups based on how the head and leaves are formed, and within those groups there are numerous varieties. Crisphead is a group of lettuce like iceberg lettuce, with a tightly formed, pale green head. Romaine, or cos, is used mainly for salads and sandwiches. This group forms long, upright heads, and is the basis for Caesar salads. Looseleaf lettuces are very loose in form, and leaves will sometimes grow again when they are cut back. They come in a wide variety of colors and may have speckles and frilly edges. Batavians, also referred to as Summercrisps or French crisps, have a form that is not as tight as a crisphead but not as loose as the looseleaf group. Butterhead, also known as Boston or Bibb lettuce, forms a head, though it is a looser head than iceberg or crispheads. It is very sweet and tender.

GROWING Lettuces are one of the few edible crops that can tolerate some shade. In fact, they do really well underplanted in dappled shade provided by taller plants such as tomatoes or pole beans. They are easily seeded into flowerpots or the vegetable garden. Cover the seeds with a dusting of soil or organic compost, pat gently with the palm of your hand, and water in carefully. Keep evenly moist. Lettuces will mature in 40 to 60 days, depending on the individual variety. For a jumpstart in the spring or in the fall when you have some bare spots in the garden, look for six-packs of lettuce starts and tuck them in where space allows. Plant at the same depth they were in the package.

Lettuce has lots of admirers, including many garden inhabitants who love it as much as we do. Cutworms, wireworms, leafhoppers, aphids, slugs, snails, rabbits and ground squirrels act as though you laid out a picnic for them. Floating row covers from garden centers may come in handy to protect your lettuces from the chompers. And remember, rather than just chopping a whole head of lettuce, it is very important to wash every leaf under cold running water, front and back, carefully, to get rid of grit and passengers.

HARVESTING Different types of lettuce will be harvested according to their form. For lettuce that makes heads, harvest the whole head with a sharp knife at the base of the head. Leaf lettuces can be cut with a knife. Many lettuces, particularly the loose-leaf varieties, may be considered cut-and-come-again, meaning that when they are just 4 to 5 inches tall, you can cut them off just 2 inches above the soil, and a second flush of growth will appear in a few days for another harvest.

The beauty of lettuce is that it can be harvested almost throughout the year, until it starts to bolt, and you will know when that is near because the plants begin to shoot up vertically, send out little yellow or white flowers, and the leaves become bitter. Remove the tired plants and reseed a fresh crop.

VARIETIES I recommend that you try several lettuce cultivars to decide which ones do best in your growing conditions, which aesthetically appeal to you, and which ones taste best to you. Many have captivating names: **Flashy Trout's Back** (27 days) and **Freckles** (28 to 55 days, depending on size desired) are varieties of romaine lettuce; **Tango** (53 days) is a frilly looseleaf lettuce; and **Green Deer Tongue** (50 days) and **Tennis Ball** (55 days) are both Bibb types. Lettuce looseleaf blends labeled cut-and-come-again have names like Italian salad mix and mesclun (21 to 30 days) salad mix and include some spicy items like radishes, **Mâche** (ready in 50 days and will overwinter in warmer valley regions), or Asian mustard greens. **Parris Island Cos** (68 days), a romaine, is dandy for Caesar salads.

Onions

Onions are a staple in most pantries, and easy to grow in the Rocky Mountain garden. For this discussion, we make a distinction between the big, sweet onions, and the "hard," "storage," or "keeper" onions. All onions love our long days and sunshine, and both types do very well here. The so-called "sweets" have a high water content and a very mild flavor, making them good for eating raw. But that high moisture content means they do not store well—maybe a couple months at best. The keeper or storage onions, generally Spanish and white bulbous onions, have thicker skins, lower water content, and store well under dry, cool conditions. White onions, milder than Spanish but with some zing, are preferred in Mexican cuisine. Red onions are somewhere between the sweets and the keepers, and are popular for salads.

GROWING Given well-drained but evenly moist soils and plenty of organic matter, onions can develop into baseball-size orbs. Work in some organic compost before planting. Make sure the area is free of weeds and especially grass. Bulbous onions will grow 4 to 6 inches in diameter.

HARVESTING When onions are harvested, they should be dug up and laid out in dry shade for a couple of days, to allow the skins to "cure," making them ready for storage. They should be stored in a cool, dark, dry place with good air circulation.

VARIETIES The jumbo **Walla Walla** onions (110 to 125 days) are famous sweet slicing summer onions; **Siskiyou Sweet** is a strain of the Walla Walla. **Ailsa Craig** or **Yellow Ebenezer** (105 days) is good for fresh eating. For keepers, plant Fiesta, **Utah Yellow Sweet Spanish** (110 days) or **Mustang** (108 days). **Red Zeppelin** is a red storage onion, often holding well for up to 8 months. They are large, pretty, and excellent for our region (110 days). Purchase only certified onion sets or plants grown from certified seed (see page 220).

Parsnips

Sweet, buttery, and a tad spicy, parsnips are a delicious member of the carrot family. One of the few vegetables that improves with age, they can be left in the ground until the following spring. Just be sure to mulch them or compost to protect them from deep frosts. Oven-roasted with olive oil and salt, parsnips are scrumptious.

GROWING Give parsnips fertile, well-drained, sandy soil in full sun to which plenty of compost has been added—as much as 3 to 4 inches layered on top, then worked into the bed. Like for all root crops, a fine soil, free of lumps and rocks, will produce the straightest and tastiest parsnips. The roots can plunge up to 20 inches, so work the soil deeply. Direct seed as soon as the soil is tillable, planting ½ inch deep. Sprinkle a few radish seeds with each parsnip seed to help break up the crust of the soil and to divert insects. Parsnips may take as long as three weeks to germinate. Keep the area free of weeds, since parsnips resent the competition. Thin to one plant every 6 inches, with rows 18 inches apart.

HARVESTING They grow very deeply, so harvest with care. Gently dig them with a spading fork. They can be stored in a cool, dark, dry root cellar. The sweetest flavor is achieved by leaving them in the ground at least two weeks after the first hard frost.

VARIETIES **Harris Model**, **Hollow Crown**, and **All American** are recommended heirloom varieties (95 to 110 days).

Peas

The delight of spring, peas are incredibly easy to grow and are at their absolute finest when eaten within minutes of being harvested. There are three types to know: garden or English peas, snow peas, and sugar snap peas. Most varieties are available in a shorter bush type, as well as a tall and vining type. The garden pea is shelled before eating, the snow peas are grown for their tender, flat pods, and the sugar snap pea is a hybrid that can be eaten whole, with fat peas inside a sweet, crunchy, edible pod. Peas are a great crop for the coolest parts of our region, and succession crops can be planted every two weeks.

GROWING Peas do best in cool weather; and can withstand damp (not waterlogged) spring conditions, so they are among the first vegetables you can plant out in the garden. Give all types something to grow on. Perhaps the cheapest and best method I've used for supporting shorter varieties is to use the red- and yellow-twig dogwood branches pruned from elsewhere in my garden. Pod peas, like snow peas and snap peas, can grow to 6 feet, so give them a net or taller stakes to climb up. As soon as the ground can be worked, sow peas in a 3-inch-deep trench, 1 inch apart, and cover with ½ inch of soil lightly tamped down over them. Rows should be 2 feet apart. Depending on the variety, provide support stakes or netting for your peas. After planting, water in gently, from below. If the weather cooperates, you may not have to offer much supplemental water.

HARVESTING Garden peas should be harvested when the pods have just started to fill out; if you wait too long, they will be inedible. Occasionally open a pod to check on them. Pea pod types (snow peas and snap peas) should be harvested when they are about 3 inches long. Be careful to not tear the vine: hold the pod in one hand and the stem in the other, and carefully tug on the pea pod to remove it.

VARIETIES **Golden India** (70 days) is a beautiful tall yellow snow pea, at 6 feet. **Little Marvel** (62 days), a garden pea, forms a bush only 18 to 20 inches tall, while **Green Arrow** (68 days), also a garden pea, is between 24 to 28 inches. **Sugar Snap** (that's its name) is a delicious cross between a garden pea and a pea pod variety. It will grow to 6 feet and can be harvested in 62 days. **Dwarf Gray Sugar Snap** (60 days), an heirloom variety, grows 24 inches tall.

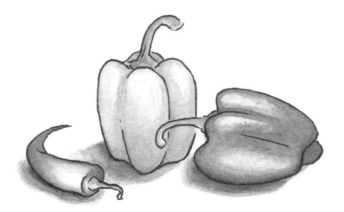

Peppers

Here's a fun little ditty about peppers: "In 1493, Columbus took peppers across the sea." He did, and they caught on like wildfire in Europe. At one point, while the Spanish were busy invading Mexico, jalapeño peppers could be used to pay your taxes. Both sweet and hot peppers are used extensively in today's kitchen, and growing your own will enable you to try varieties that are hard to find in the market. Growing hot peppers has become so popular in our country, a magazine and catalog are devoted to the subject. Sweet peppers can be temperamental in our intermountain gardens, but you should give them a try anyway. The fruits of sweet peppers can be green (immature), yellow, red, purple, orange, brown, and pale white as well as in a variety of shapes and sizes. The plants themselves can be 24 to 36 inches tall and 20 inches wide.

GROWING Sweet or hot peppers—all come under the heading of hotties in terms of vegetable gardening—they like full sun and warm weather. Easily grown from seed, they should be started indoors six weeks before the last frost date in your area. Transplants are set out when the soil is warm, and given regular, deep watering. To warm the soil before you plant, mulch with black plastic, and add lots of organic mulch after the soil is ready.

HARVESTING Peppers come in every size and shape, so refer to the seed packet or plant tag to know exactly when to pick. Use gloves to harvest hot peppers such as jalapeño, habanero, and Scotch bonnets, since most people are sensitive to the oils in peppers, which give a hot, painful sensation. A pair of garden scissors is handy for cutting the pepper cleanly from the plant.

VARIETIES **Jalapeño** (65 to 80 days) is hot and zingy, well known, and a favorite in salsas. **Pasilla** (85 days) is a standard medium-hot pepper from Mexico that turns dark brown after it ripens. It is used extensively in Tex-Mex cooking. The hot and sassy **Fish** pepper (80 days) is an African heirloom, a 2-foot-tall plant bearing 3-inch colorful striped peppers. **Buran Sweet** (90 days) is a brilliant, almost hot pink sweet pepper variety, and **Yellow Banana Sweet** (78 days) is a delicious and mild heirloom. Red or yellow, **Corno di Toro** (72 days) is not hot at all, but a sweet, long fryer from Italy. Frying peppers are eaten raw but are at their most delicious when sautéed in olive oil until tender. **Jimmy Nardello** (75 days) frying pepper is a sweet Italian variety.

Potatoes

A crop with a rich, poignant history of emigration and heartache, the potato still graces some Idaho license plates. While it's hard to beat a classic Idaho spud— the finest of which are large and smoothly shaped with a slightly rough skin texture, called "netting" or "russet"—there are dozens of other varieties, colors, shapes, sizes, and textures to choose from and they grow well in the organic home garden. Fingerling potatoes are long and narrow, as the name implies, while "new potatoes" are baby potatoes of any potato variety, harvested early when the skin is paper-thin.

GROWING Potatoes, a member of the nightshade family, take a bit of effort to grow well but the effort pays off handsomely. Dig a trench in the garden, about 6 inches wide and as deep. Place your certified seed potato pieces, sprouts up, 12 inches apart, and cover with 3 inches of soil. As the plants grow, and when 3 to 4 inches high, cover the stem with more soil. Potatoes can also be grown in tall, well-drained boxes, cages, and fiber sacks made especially for home gardening applications. Apply at least 1 to 2 inches of water a week all at once, and water regularly for shapely potatoes.

HARVESTING When the flowers have faded and the potato plant turns yellow, about ten weeks after planting, the potatoes are ready for harvesting. Refer to the growing instructions for each variety, and harvest when they are at the recommended size. To check, carefully dig down about 8 inches away from the plant stem, and feel around for a tuber. Brush off the soil, but don't wash before cooking. For storage, keep in a dark place, with excellent air circulation, that is cool but not freezing. If exposed to light, they will develop a green discoloration, making them mildly toxic so no longer edible.

VARIETIES The famous **Idaho Russet** potato (120 days) is especially well suited for baking, frying, and mashing. **Red Pontiac** (80 to 100 days) is an excellent heirloom variety, mid-season, with red skin, a good keeper, and is best for boiling. The waxy, dense texture of **Yukon Gold** (70 to 85 days) makes it an excellent choice for steaming, boiling, and potato salads (I like it especially for scalloped potatoes) For sheer novelty of appearance, try blue potatoes: **Adirondack Blue** and **All Blue** (90 to 105 days). A tasty fingerling heirloom, **Rose Finn Apple** (105 to 135 days) has blush skin, yellow flesh, and is a good keeper.

Radishes

I have a special fondness for radishes because they were the first vegetable I grew. The heart-shaped leaves that appear in just 7 to 10 days are so gratifying for the young gardener. Spicy, mild, hot, crispy, and cool, all adjectives can be applied to the radish family. We often don't realize the usefulness and versatility of the radish. In Europe, thinly sliced radishes are served on fresh, buttered bread as a salad. They can be added to any sandwich to add crunch and zing. And remember, you don't always need lettuce to make a salad—slice up a bowl of radishes, dress them simply with a bit of rice vinegar and salt and fresh pepper, let them sit a while and you have a refreshing simple dinner salad.

GROWING Direct sow radish seeds, covering them with just ¼ inch of soil. Plant a crop every two or three weeks for a constant harvest. The large storage-type radishes, such as daikon, do very well in cool areas, parts of Wyoming, Montana, and Colorado, and can be planted late July or early August for a fall harvest.

HARVESTING Inspect a radish's "shoulders" to see if it is mature enough to harvest. This will depend on each variety, so consult the seed packet. When thinning out the plantings, use thinnings for the dinner salad: they add a zippy flavor.

VARIETIES **Chinese Red Meat**, **Beauty Heart**, or **Watermelon Radish** (all the same radish; 55 days) will grow up to 3 inches in diameter. **Japanese Daikon** (50 days) is a huge one, weighing in at 2 to 6 pounds and growing 2 feet long! **Petite French Breakfast** (20 to 25 days) radishes are oblong, red, with white tips. **Cherry Belle** (25 days) is a classic red, nonpithy variety. Look for newly resurrected striking heirloom varieties like **Black Spanish** (with rough black skin, spicy white flesh) and **Hilds Blauer** (purple outside, white inside), which both mature in 55 days and prefer cool weather.

Raspberries

Raspberries are fragile, perfumed, richly colored jewels of the garden. Their name alone can make you recall their heady fragrance. Is there anything better than a bowl of fresh, warm raspberries with a splash of cream and a dusting of sugar? Their fragility makes them near impossible to ship, so the best way to ensure an abundance of raspberries is to make space to grow your own.

GROWING Raspberries come in two basic types: summer bearing and ever-bearing. Summer bearing will produce one large crop, generally in late June or around the first of July. Ever-bearing actually have two crops, one in early summer and one in the fall. Ever-bearing varieties are not a good choice for towns with short growing seasons, since you may well have frost before they set fruit. Raspberries, generally speaking, if planted in the right place, with proper moisture and air circulation, will grow like weeds. They are hardy enough for McCall, Idaho, and other mile-high towns and gardens in our region. Since raspberries have no prickly thorns, they are picker friendly.

Make it a rule to keep your raspberries in rows, and make the rows only 18 inches wide. The rows can be as long as space allows. Make it a priority to keep the canes inside their row. The best way to maintain a raspberry patch is to prune it in the early spring, before the buds appear. Cut to the ground any canes with gray, peeling bark, and those that are thin and spindly. Remove any "suckers," or any plants that sprout up outside the designated growing area. Thin the remaining canes, leaving just three or four per square foot. It is easy to tell old canes from new canes, because the old canes have tired-looking bark that generally turns gray and there may be some old, dried-up berries clinging to the canes. New canes will be flexible and bright and should be topped off at 4 to 5 feet. The first time you thin your raspberry patch it will look sparse, but don't worry. Add a couple of inches of organic compost to the row every spring: the compost will add to the soil as well as help retain moisture as a mulch. Raspberries benefit from being supported on both sides by a taut, stout wire, strung between two strong poles at the ends of the rows.

Canes bear only once, then you remove them and put in

new canes. A well-maintained raspberry patch will continue to produce for years.

Any well-drained soil is good for raspberries. Different varieties have different pruning requirements, so be sure to know what variety you purchased and get the accompanying instructions (or check online) for the correct techniques for your specific plants. If at all possible, plant both summer- and fall-bearing for extended harvests.

Adequate water is needed for good fruit development. Check the soil 6 to 9 inches below the surface: Moist and cool is what you want. Water deeply and thoroughly before the ground freezes in late autumn. Hot, dry weather brings spider mites, so wash them off with a burst of water from the hose nozzle.

HARVESTING Berries are ripe when they are plump and fully shaped. They should slip easily from the plant.

VARIETIES **Boyne**, an early to midseason red variety, originated in Manitoba and is extra hardy for our coldest areas. **Nova** is also a red midseason variety, renowned for its disease resistant qualities. **Latham**, a well-known and reliable red cultivar, is very long lived and tasty. It is ready midsummer. **Heritage**, a red variety, is another popular type in our region. It's easy to find and grow, and good for jams and freezing. **Anne** and **Fall Gold**, both yellow fruiting, dazzle people who've not seen a golden raspberry. While the flavor is not as intense as for its red cousins, it is very sweet and good for eating fresh. In Boise, Fall Gold will fruit until the hardest frost in October. Colorado State University research shows Nova, Boyne, and fall-bearing varieties are well suited to gardens on Colorado's Front Range, and on the western slope, you can grow both ever-bearing and summer raspberries.

Rhubarb

This classic, old-timey perennial garden fruit is technically a vegetable. You'll find rhubarb plants in most established, large veggie gardens—they are incredibly long-lived and capable of surviving neglect and abandonment. The crispy, red, green, pink, or speckled pink stalks are in high demand. The leaves, however, are poisonous, so cut them off before using the stalks.

GROWING The best time to plant is early spring, when crowns, or rootstock, are available at local nurseries. Find a place to plant the rhubarb where it can grow undisturbed for a long, long time. Give each plant plenty of space: at least 3 feet in every direction. The planting hole should be amended with a few handfuls of organic compost, and the crown set 2 inches below the final soil level of the garden bed. Carefully backfill with soil, and water in well.

Rhubarb needs four to six hours of sun every day. Considered a heavy feeder, it loves to be planted in rich soil and to get an annual or twice-yearly top dressing of good organic compost. Add a bucket of compost all around the crown of the plant after it has finished producing stalks for the year, and once again in the fall when you put the vegetable garden to bed for the winter.

Rhubarb plants prefer to be undisturbed, but kept free of encroaching grass and weeds. Cut the tall flower stalk from the center as soon as it starts to appear. This will keep the plant's energy where it needs it most—in the root system. Rhubarb likes a well-drained soil and even moisture, but it will survive with very little human intervention.

HARVESTING The first year you plant rhubarb, you must just sit and watch it grow. You can remove the tall flower stalk when it shows up, tall and prominent. The second year, watch for the stalks to turn a deep, red color (or for some varieties, a green color) and to reach up to 1 inch in diameter. With a sharp knife, cut the stalk cleanly at the base. Rhubarb can be harvested without a knife, but be careful when pulling a stalk from the crown so you don't tear the plant. In the second year and after, leave behind several stalks so the plant will have a way to rejuvenate itself.

VARIETIES Rhubarb is a perennial and all varieties take two years to reach a harvestable size. **Crimson Cherry** (also known as **Crimson Wine**, **Crimson Red**, or just **Crimson**) is among the reddest of rhubarbs, perfect for making rhubarb jam, pie, compote, and juice. **Valentine** is vigorous, sporting thick red stalks that hold their color well when cooked. It produces few or no flower/seed stalks. **Victoria** is known for its sweet stalks—long, round, and smooth—which are not tough or stringy and have a rich flavor. This variety sends up an enormous flower stalk. **Canada Red**, available in the Canadian provinces, yields juicy stalks that are cherry-red throughout, and keeps that beautiful red color after cooking. And the Canadian pink **MacDonald** is a tried and true performer in the coldest of parts of our region. If you can, get your hands on a cultivar named **German Wine**—the speckled green stalks are similar in taste to Victoria but even more vigorous.

Rutabagas and Turnips

There are turnips, an ancient root crop from Siberia, with a white bulb shape and purple shoulders, and then there are rutabagas. You may sometimes hear rutabagas referred to by their old name, "swedes." Rutabagas are a type of yellow turnip with purple shoulders, hailing from Scandinavia. They are larger than turnips, a bit coarser in appearance, and have a slightly stronger flavor. Turnip leaves are delicious lightly steamed as greens. When planning your crop rotation, remember that these two root vegetables are members of the cabbage (brassica) family.

GROWING Some gardeners grow turnips in the spring, and then grow rutabagas as a fall crop since they hold well over the winter. Sow turnips early in the spring, ½ to 1 inch deep, as soon as the garden soil can be worked. Thin turnips to 4 inches apart and rutabagas to 6 inches.

HARVESTING Turnips and rutabagas should be about 3 inches in diameter at harvest. Before harvesting the root, you can snip and use some of the leaves from both vegetables, but be sure to leave a few on each plant so it can continue to develop. For rutabagas, if possible wait until there have been a couple light frosts before harvesting, since the cold temperatures will increase their sweet flavor.

VARIETIES **Golden Globe** turnip (55 days) is highly resistant to the root maggot, sometimes a problem with both turnips and swedes, and is best harvested with 3 inches in diameter. **Purple Top Globe** turnip (55 days) should be harvested when 3 to 4 inches in diameter. **Joan** rutabaga (90 to 100 days) is an **American Purple Top** rutabaga with smooth, round, uniform roots. The dense, yellow flesh is crispy with a sweet, mild flavor that improves after frost. It is a good keeper.

Shallots

Shallots are a perennial onion—actually a multiplier onion—easily grown in our part of the country and adored by gourmet cooks for their subtle, complex flavor—like a mild onion with a hint of garlic. They are called multipliers or perennials because a single planted bulb will produce as many as 8 to 12 more bulbs. Hardy in zones 2 to 9, shallots have pinkish brown skin and pale purple flesh. Look for "sets"— small bulbils ready for planting—in the spring at your local garden center. Purchase only certified onion sets (see page 220).

GROWING Plant individual bulbs pointy end up, 6 inches apart, just below the soil line. As with all members of the allium family, they like well-drained, amended soil. Water evenly and deeply once a week. When harvesting, gently dig each cluster and separate into individual pieces shallots.

HARVESTING Dig up and cure before storing. In many places, shallots can be left in the ground over the winter and will start growing again in the spring.

VARIETIES Look for those labeled **French Grey**, **Ambition**, or **Prisma** (all 110 days).

Spinach

Once upon a time, farmers gave the Popeye cartoon series credit for increasing the sales of spinach by as much as 30 percent. Nowadays, spinach doesn't need a front man; everyone knows it's chock full of nutrition and must-have minerals. Like lettuce mixes and chard, spinach can be tucked in almost anywhere you have a bit of space. Just remember to water it in the dry season.

GROWING Spinach and its spinach-flavored cousins—which look very much like spinach and often the only way to tell them all apart is by their botanical names—are very easy to grow. In the hottest parts of the west, there is probably a variety you can grow, even with a bit of shade. It will actually survive subzero temperatures, so this green is for you folks in the high country. Direct sow the seeds at ½ inch deep and 1 inch apart in rows or scatter them carefully across a wide flower pot. As with the other greens, as the leaves emerge, thin the plants, snacking as you go. You will want the plants to be about 4 to 6 inches apart to develop into something other than baby spinach leaves. Keep the soil evenly moist but not soggy. When winter comes, a 2- to 4-inch layer of organic mulch, clean leaves, or a light sheet of garden fabric (row cover) will protect it. Mark the spinach bed with a stake so you can find it under the snow.

HARVESTING Garden scissors or pruners will give you a clean cut when harvesting spinach. Cut near the soil and base of the plant. With New Zealand spinach, at 4 inches tall, trim the leaves and another crop will follow. Malabar spinach, a climbing variety, is snipped from the vines.

VARIETIES Several varieties do well in our region. **Bloomsdale** (40 to 60 days) is time tested and reliable, with very good yields. **LaVewa** (28 to 45 days) is an heirloom spinach with smooth leaves and a rich flavor. Since spinach proper (of the genus *Spinacia*) doesn't much care for the heat in places like Boise, Salt Lake, or Reno, gardeners have the option of filling in with near-spinach alternatives: either New Zealand spinach (genus *Tetragonia*) or Malabar spinach (genus *Basella*). **Malabar** (85 days) has gorgeous deep red vines, so let it scamper up a trellis in a pot on the patio or plant it to grow where the peas once held court. **New Zealand** spinach (50 to 85 days) may be slow to germinate; soak seeds overnight before planting.

Squash (Summer)

Summer squash come in many colors and shapes. The most common cultivars, such as zucchini and yellow crookneck, have fruit that is green, yellow, or white, and are round, straight, club shaped, and patty shaped (the patty pan type). There is even an heirloom trombone-shaped climbing zucchini!

GROWING Summer squash need only about 40 to 60 days to produce a bumper crop. Dry, sunny weather is critical for good pollination, though drought will reduce fruit set. Bush varieties are a well-contained choice for smaller gardens. Plant seeds of bush varieties 2 feet apart in rows 5 feet apart. With the hill method, create a raised hill 48 inches in diameter, plant three to five seeds, and thin to two or three plants when they have their first set of leaves. Squash bugs can ruin a crop in very little time; remove by hand picking. Squash foliage likes to stay dry, so water from below.

HARVESTING We've all heard stories of gardens and gardeners overrun by their prolific zucchini plants. Once they get going, they grow so fast it is hard to keep up with them. Be sure to check for squash under the leaves of the plant—every day. Pick 2 to 8 days after bloom when the fruit is 4 to 8 inches long, 2 inches in diameter (3 to 4 inches for patty pan), and when the rind is still soft.

VARIETIES Zucchini types include the small-fruited heirloom **Tatuma** (50 days); **8 Ball** and **Cue Ball** (40 to 45 days) are both early, baseball size, and especially good grilled. The heirloom zucchini, **Costata Romanesco** (54 days), is an Italian variety that wins all taste tests. It also has a distinctive appearance with its pronounced ridges. **Tromboncino** (80 days) is fun to grow because the zucchini squash are trombone shaped and the fruit itself will grow up to 3 feet long; grow it on a trellis. **Early Prolific Straightneck** (50 to 55 days) is a prized heirloom yellow summer squash. **Gold Rush** and **Goldbar** (both 50 to 55 days) are zucchini-type, hybrid, golden, straightneck squash. **Sundance** (50 to 55 days) is a flavorful, golden summer crookneck squash. Favorite patty pan squashes include **Scallopini** (52 days), which is both green and yellow; **White Scallop** (55 to 60 days), an early American Indian squash; and the beautiful **Pattison Striped** (60 to 75 days) French heirloom.

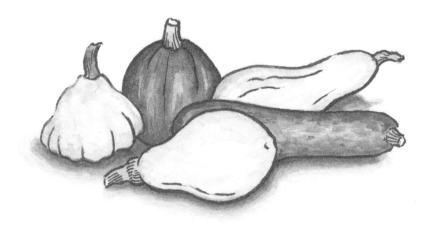

Squash (Winter) and Pumpkins

I have a crush on pumpkins and winter squash. If I had an acre, we'd be growing about thirty different varieties—some just for their good looks and names. If they won't fit in the garden proper, consider the wild edges of your lawn or along the driveway. These are serious winter keepers. And wouldn't you know, they just happen to be loaded with beta-carotene and fiber, the stuff wholesome good diets are made of.

GROWING Like summer squash, winter squash and pumpkins are quick to germinate and easy to grow, so don't even think of planting them until you are sure you've seen the last frost of the season. Best direct sown into the garden and planted in hills, they need lots of space. If you are growing the jumbo-sized varieties, give them their own space. Allow 4 to 6 feet between mounds, and drip irrigation is the appropriate and most efficient method for watering the plants.

To grow nutritious squash, start with a good soil, to which you have added large amounts of organic compost. Since they are heavy feeders, I recommend regular (every two weeks) supplemental feedings of seaweed fertilizer or another organic water-soluble fertilizer. If you are growing pumpkins competitively, thin to just one pumpkin per vine.

HARVESTING When you plant the seeds for these, make a note on your calendar, and flip through the pages until you have come to the 100-day mark, and make a potential harvesting note. Depending on the weather, your squash should be maturing nicely by this point.

VARIETIES **Big Max** and **Atlantic Giant** (120 days plus) pumpkins are the ones to plant if you are going for the whopper-size prize winners. If a fairytale coach is more your style, check out the gorgeous, deeply lobed, **Rouge Vif d'Etampes** or **French Cinderella** pumpkin (110 days); it happens to be delicious, too. **Small Sugar** is an heirloom pumpkin popular for cooking because of its fine, sweet, flavorful flesh (95 to 105 days). **Blue Hubbard** winter squash is one of the finest keepers, with a somewhat warty blue-gray skin; they weigh between 15 and 30 pounds. Fine textured, sweet, delicious flesh is your reward for growing these. **Red Kuri** (95 days) may be the best flavored of all the winter squash; the color is deep red orange and it bakes up beautifully. This variety is reliable for cooler areas with short seasons. I've got to mention **Blue Jarrahdale** (100 days), the slate-skinned, orange-fleshed pumpkin, simply because it is gorgeous. It is delicious and a good keeper, therefore useful as well as ornamental.

Strawberries

Delicious, fragrant, juicy strawberries are a garden-er's dream. There are tiny, wild alpine berries that will self-seed throughout a garden or perennial bed, as well as ever-bearing, June-bearing, and French market varieties. For some vegetable gardeners, the venerable strawberry is the only fruit they grow. To stand in your garden, eating fresh strawberries off the plant, is true heaven.

GROWING Plant strawberries in a warm microclimate area in your garden so they are protected from damaging late-spring frosts. They need full sun and prefer loose soil that has been amended with organic matter. Creating slightly raised rows or hills will improve drainage. A layer of mulch around those hills and between the rows will keep weeds at bay and help retain valuable moisture. Create raised beds or rows about 4 inches high. If you don't have much bed space to dedicate to strawberries, plants do well in special strawberry pots that are made with bulging pockets to accommodate their growth, or in large container pots with at least 12 inches of rich soil.

Strawberry plants need to be placed carefully in the soil with the crowns planted exactly at soil level (see the illustration on page 77). Strawberries have shallow root systems so they need to be kept moist: water regularly, every couple of days. This is critical during fruiting and again in the fall when the plants ready themselves for the next season.

Strawberry plantings need to be rejuvenated in the fall, after they have been growing a couple of years. Strawberry plants are productive for three years at most. But you don't need to buy replacements, since the mother plant sends out new plants ("daughters") to keep the goodness coming.

HARVESTING Strawberries have a marvelous way of telling you when they are ready to pick: they glow bright red and taste fabulous. Anything less is just not ready. Simple enough?

VARIETIES Ever-bearing strawberries produce two crops in one season: one in June to July and another in late summer, July to August. These are not recommended for short-season areas in our region. **Ogallala** is the hardiest of this type with a very good flavor. **Fort Laramie**, a heavy producer, is a day-neutral type, meaning it will ripen no matter how many daylight hours it gets. "Day neutral" is essentially the same as "ever-bearing." The Fort Laramie strawberry was developed in Cheyenne, Wyoming, so it is especially suited for that part of our region. June-bearing varieties produce the largest fruit, but only one crop per year, in June or early July. **Honeoye** is a robust, flavorful, large fruited early bearing plant. **Sparkle**, an old-time favorite for jam making, is generally ripe in July, with excellent flavor. **Allstar** is another July gem, a large berry resistant to verticillium wilt (see page 43).

Day-neutral strawberries produce all season. In the coldest parts of the Rockies, day neutrals are an excellent choice. Remove all the blossoms the first month after planting, then let them produce, harvesting the berries until a hard frost. **Tribute** offers up plenty of large fruits midseason. **Tristar** has medium fruit, and does well even in heavy soils. Both are resistant to verticillium wilt. In a flavor class by itself, but also day-neutral, the **Mara des Bois** French strawberry may be difficult to find, is usually only available through mail order, very expensive, and worth every penny. It has exquisite wild flavor and large berry size—a perfect combination. In my garden in Boise, Mara des Bois is an excellent producer, slowing down only during the hottest part of the summer.

Tomatoes

Tomatoes are the most widely grown of all the vegetable garden plants. There are contests for first tomato, ugliest tomato, smallest tomato, largest tomato, prettiest tomato, and, of course, the best-tasting tomato. With hundreds of varieties to choose from, everyone has their own favorite best performers for where they live. There seem to be new, different tomatoes appearing at the market every year. Just when you think you've seen it all, along comes a blue tomato from Oregon!

Perhaps the biggest revolution in growing tomatoes has been the resurgence of the heirloom varieties for the home garden. Especially well suited to individual tastes, too fragile to ship, exceptionally high in vitamins, best eaten warm, these beloved traditional varieties have taken the garden scene by storm. They are very juicy and full of flavor—and have distinctly different flavors—as well as being incredibly colorful with interesting shapes. There is an heirloom tomato for every garden.

GROWING Tomatoes can be started from seed, but they need plenty of light, good air circulation, and consistently warm temperatures to flourish. Transplants are the preferred method for starting tomatoes in our unpredictable climate. The soil should be warm and the last frost past. Place each transplant 24 inches apart in each direction, in fertile soil, in full sun. You can plant them deep enough to cover the first set of leaves on the stem, but remove those leaves that would be buried before you plant. Make a small moat around each plant to hold water.

Soaker hoses are the best way to deliver water to the plants. Hot caps, cloches, row covers, and other season extenders are employed to grow tomatoes in areas with unpredictable frost patterns. Polar fleece is an effective cover. Tomatoes should be supported or staked. These big plants have big root systems. Regular, deep watering is critical. Be sure to check the plants if is blazingly hot. The single best way to test for adequate moisture is to take a trowel, dig down to about 8 inches (without damaging the roots). This soil should be moist, but not soggy. Too little or too much water will result in an imbalance of calcium in the plant causing blossom end rot as well as poor fruit production. Blossom end rot is not a disease, but an imbalance in the plant's uptake of nutrients. The tomatoes (as well as squash, peppers, cucumbers and melons) will develop an unsightly round leathery brown patch on the bottom of the fruit. Sometimes this will occur when the plants are set out when the soil is too cold or when the garden season begins wet and dries out very quickly. Failure to get the watering right results in blossom end rot and poor fruit production. Nasty hornworms should be removed by hand and disposed of.

HARVESTING You know when the tomatoes are ripe, because you will have been staring at them, hoping they would hurry up and redden. Tomatoes ripen from the first on the branch outward. Look under the leaves, where some may be hiding. Use two hands to pick each tomato: one to hold the branch and one to break off the tomato at the stem notch. Tomatoes are too ripe when the flesh is soft and mushy.

VARIETIES Tomatoes plants come in three primary growing types: determinate, indeterminate, and of course to confuse everyone, semi-indeterminate. The easiest way to keep them straight is to think of the determinate ones as "determined" to produce. They do, all in one big blush of fruits. These are well suited for people who want to can their produce in a short period of time. After this big effort, the plants—generally bushy and short in stature—start to deteriorate. Indeterminate types, and these include most of the heirloom and open-pollinated cultivars, will yield fruit over a very long period. They are often slow to start ripening but once they get going, they will blossom and fruit until the first hard frost. They must be staked to work well in narrow garden beds. Always check the label or the plant tag to know which type you are getting.

The new kid on the block, **Indigo Rose**, is an open-pollinated, indeterminate variety (70 days). It is deep purple to reddish orange and is perfect for salads. The folks who developed it claim it is the first improved tomato variety with anthocyanins (blue antioxidant genes). **Red Oxheart** is an indeterminate (80 to 85 days) often yielding extra large, 1 pound, solid, heart-shaped fruits with old-fashioned flavor. **Siberian**, of Russian descent, is semi-indeterminate (48 days), and will produce 3- to 5-ounce fruits. It will set fruit in cool weather, is known to be very early ripening, and a great choice for high-country gardens with short growing seasons. **Stupice** is an indeterminate (52 days) with 1- to 2-ounce fruits. A small Czechoslovakian tomato, it is very early, cold tolerant, with a sweet, tangy flavor and amazingly high yields (average 87 fruits per plant). **Costoluto Genovese** is a semi-indeterminate (80 days) lobed Italian heirloom with an earthy, old-fashioned flavor. When sliced, the scalloped edges look beautiful. **Aunt Ruby's German Green** will give you 12- to 16-ounce green beefsteak fruits with delicious sweet flavor. Fruits are light green at maturity, flushed with a little pink. It has an indeterminate growth habit (80 days). **Mortgage Lifter**, the famous beefsteak heirloom indeterminate (75 to 85 days) with enormous 1- to 4-pound fruits, is a perfect sandwich tomato. It produces smooth, pink-skinned fruits even in droughts. **Sun Gold** is another small, indeterminate type, with bright orange-gold ½-ounce fruits ready in just 57 days. These cherry tomatoes, which are borne in trusses, are exceptionally sweet. This tomato will not stop producing until the plant is killed by frost.

Resources

The sheer size and breadth of the mountain states region makes it impossible to address every microclimate, pest issue, or soil conundrum folks may encounter in their gardens. As we participate in this ancient rewarding ritual of gardening, it's good to know we have many excellent and informative resources at our fingertips. Please dig deep into these recommended databases, and talk with local experts for ongoing support and information.

CLIMATE AND WEATHER INFORMATION

Hardiness zone map (USDA) for the United States
www.usna.usda.gov/Hardzone/ushzmap.html

Hardiness zone maps for Canada
www.planthardiness.gc.ca/
www.plantmaps.com/interactive-canada-hardiness-gardening-zone-map.php

The Drought Monitor
www.droughtmonitor.unl.edu/
Updated weekly, the maps rely on information from multiple sources compiled by federal and academic scientists.

National Oceanic and Atmospheric Administration, U.S. Climate Normals
www.ncdc.noaa.gov/oa/climate/normals/usnormals.html
NOAA's National Climatic Data Center offers state-by-state averages for 1981 to 2010 of first and last frost dates, growing degree dates, and more.

National Phenology Network
www.usanpn.org/home
Citizens and scientists together, studying the impact of climate change on our ecosystems.

SOIL TESTING LABORATORIES

Soil and Plant Laboratory
San Jose, CA
www.soilandplantlaboratory.com

Stukenholtz Laboratory
Twin Falls, ID
www.stukenholtz.com

SEED AND PLANT SUPPLIERS

Abundant Life Seeds
Cottage Grove, Oregon
www.abundantlifeseeds.com
Certified organic and biodynamic
seeds along with OMRI listed fertilizers
and pest controls.

Adaptive Seeds
Sweet Home, Oregon
www.adaptiveseeds.com
Rare, diverse, and resilient seed
varieties adapted to short-season
northern climates.

Baker Creek Heirloom Seeds
Mansfield, Missouri
www.rareseeds.com
One of America's largest providers of
nonhybrid, non-GMO, nontreated, and
nonpatented seed.

Botanical Interests
Broomfield, Colorado
www.botanicalinterests.com
Beautifully illustrated seed packets
chock-full of detailed growing
directions and inspirational
information.

Fedco Seeds
Waterville, Maine
www.fedcoseeds.com
Purveyors of high-quality, organic
seeds, many especially well suited for
cold hardiness.

Gourmet Seed International LLC
Tatum, New Mexico
www.gourmetseed.com
Hard-to-find and authentic heirloom
and gourmet vegetable and herb seed.

High Country Gardens
Santa Fe, New Mexico
www.highcountrygardens.com
Excellent pollinator plants for the
vegetable garden.

High Mowing Organic Seeds
Wolcott, Vermont
www.highmowingseeds.com
Offering 600 varieties of open-
pollinated, organic seeds.

Horizon Herbs
Williams, Oregon
www.horizonherbs.com
Offering 400 varieties of organically
grown vegetable and medicinal herb
seeds.

Hudson Valley Seed Library
Accord, New York
www.seedlibrary.org
Artful seed packets and detailed plant
information.

Irish Eyes Garden Seeds
Ellensburg, Washington
www.irisheyesgardenseeds.com
Washington-grown organic seed
potatoes and garlic, organic seed and
garden supplies.

Johnny's Selected Seeds
Waterville, Maine
www.johnnyseeds.com
Seeds include vegetables, medicinal
and culinary herbs, and cover crops;
some of the finely seeded varieties
are offered in pelletized form for
easier sowing.

Native Seeds/SEARCH
(Southwestern Endangered Arid Land
Resources Clearinghouse)
Tucson, Arizona
www.nativeseeds.org
A nonprofit seed conservation
organization offering 500 varieties of
rare and endangered ancient seeds
primarily from arid lands.

New Dimension Seed

Scappoose, Oregon

www.newdimensionseed.com

Specializing in seeds for short-season varieties of Asian vegetables.

Nichols Garden Nursery

Albany, Oregon

www.nicholsgardennursery.com

Offering vegetable, herb, and flower seeds to gardeners for more than fifty years. Extensive gardening experience in the intermountain region.

One Green World

Molalla, Oregon

www.onegreenworld.com

Bare-root cane berries and container plants of Pacific Northwest berry natives.

Osborne Seed Company

Mount Vernon, Washington

www.osborneseed.com

Organic seeds, sixteen types of radicchio and twenty-four colorful varieties of sprouting seeds.

Park Seed

Greenwood, South Carolina

www.parkseed.com

Nice selection of unusual heirloom tomatoes, beans, and squash as well as hundreds of other vegetable, herb, and flower seeds.

Peaceful Valley

Grass Valley, California

www.groworganic.com

Flower, herb, vegetable, cover crop, and sprouting seeds, as well as other garden supplies.

Pinetree Garden Seeds

New Gloucester, Maine

www.superseeds.com

A well-priced selection of heirloom vegetable seeds.

Raintree Nursery

Morton, Washington

www.raintreenursery.com

Berries, fruit trees, and a wide variety of ornamental and edible landscape plants.

Renee's Garden

Felton, California

www.reneesgarden.com

Excellent source of premixed seed blends for colorful and flavorful diversity in one packet.

Seed Savers Exchange

Decorah, Iowa

www.seedsavers.org

Nonprofit dedicated to maintaining a seed bank for heirloom seeds and plants, related educational opportunities, and a comprehensive seed catalog.

TerraEdibles

Foxboro, Ontario, Canada

www.terraedibles.ca

A wide selection of organically grown seed for popular vegetables, herbs, flowers, and aromatic sweet peas.

Territorial Seed Company

Cottage Grove, Oregon

www.territorialseed.com

Nice selection of seeds for the colder parts of our region.

Tomato Growers Supply

Fort Myers, Florida

www.tomatogrowers.com

Hundreds of varieties of tomatoes and peppers, hot chiles, sweet peppers, tomatillos and eggplants.

Veseys

York, Prince Edward Island, Canada

www.veseys.com

Veseys is a longtime supplier of seeds and other gardening supplies for gardeners in Canada as well as the United States.

Victory Seeds

Molalla, Oregon

www.victoryseeds.com

Hundreds of carefully selected, open-pollinated and heirloom vegetable seeds.

West Coast Seeds

Delta, British Columbia

www.westcoastseeds.com

Untreated non-GMO seeds for organic growing; website has a great online winter growing guide.

White Harvest Seed Company

Hartville, Missouri

www.whiteharvestseed.com

Wonderful selection of "back to the land" herb and vegetable seeds.

Wild Garden Seed

Philomath, Oregon

www.wildgardenseed.com

Organically grown, open-pollinated varieties of salad greens, vegetables, and herbs.

EXTENSION OFFICES

United States:

U.S. Department of Agriculture

www.csrees.usda.gov/Extension

Look in your local phone directory under government listings, county offices for your nearest extension office.

Colorado State University

www.ext.colostate.edu

Montana State University

www.msuextension.org

Oregon State University

www.extension.oregonstate.edu/gardening

University of Idaho

www.uidaho.edu/extension

University of Nevada

www.unce.unr.edu/programs/horticulture

Utah State University

http://extension.usu.edu/index.cfm/horticulture

Washington State University

http://gardening.wsu.edu

Wyoming

www.uwyo.edu/ces/

Canada:

Master Gardeners of Alberta Program, Edmonton

www.devonian.ualberta.ca/educationcourses/mastergardenercourse.aspx

University of Saskatchewan Master Gardener Program, Saskatoon

ccde.usask.ca/gardening

FARMERS AND FOOD BANKS

Often, after a productive garden year, you find yourself with more fresh food than you can use and want to share. Local food banks and charities welcome your produce. These national programs encourage gardeners to donate their surplus harvest to local food pantries.

Ample Harvest
www.ampleharvest.org

Local Harvest
www.localharvest.org

Plant a Row for the Hungry
www.gardenwriters.org (click on "plant a row")

Further Reading

So many books, so little time. These books are some of the ones I've turned to time and again for instruction, inspiration, and good information.

Balzer, Donna. 2012. *No Nonsense Vegetable Gardening*. St. Lynn's Press.

Carpenter, Novella. 2008. *Farm City: The Education of an Urban Farmer*. New York: Penguin.

Goldman, Amy. 2002. *Melons for the Passionate Grower*. New York: Artisan.

—. 2004. *The Compleat Squash: A Passionate Growers Guide*. New York: Artisan.

—. 2008. *The Heirloom Tomato: From Garden to Table: Recipes, Portraits, and History of the World's Most Beautiful Fruit*. New York: Bloomsbury.

Gough, Robert, and Cheryl Moore-Gough. 2011. *The Complete Guide to Saving Seeds*. North Adams, MA: Storey.

Jabbour, Niki. 2012. *The Year-Round Vegetable Gardener*. North Adams, MA: Storey, 2011.

Kingsolver, Barbara. 2007. *Animal, Vegetable, Miracle: A Year of Food Life*. New York: HarperCollins.

Lancaster, Brad. 2008. *Rainwater Harvesting for Drylands and Beyond, Vol. 1*. Tucson, Arizona: Rainsource Press.

Raven, Sarah. 2007. *The Great Vegetable Plot: Delicious Varieties to Grow and Eat*. London, England: BBC Books.

Smith, Alisa, and J. B. MacKinnon. 2008. *Plenty: One Man, One Woman, and a Raucous Year of Eating Locally*. New York: Harmony Books.

Metric Conversions

INCHES	CENTIMETERS		FEET	METERS
¼	0.6		1	0.3
½	1.3		2	0.6
¾	1.9		3	0.9
1	2.5		4	1.2
2	5.1		5	1.5
4	10		6	1.8
6	15		7	2.1
8	20		8	2.4
10	25		9	2.7
12	30		10	3
18	46		20	6
			30	9

TEMPERATURES
(DEGREES FAHRENHEIT/DEGREES CELSIUS)

$$°C = \tfrac{5}{9} \times (°F - 32)$$
$$°F = (\tfrac{9}{5} \times °C) + 32$$

VOLUME
(GALLONS/LITERS)

1	3.8
500	1892.7

Index

About the Author

Mary Ann Newcomer

Mary Ann Newcomer considers herself a garden scribe, scout, and speaker. A native Idahoan, she learned to garden in north Idaho and eastern Washington. She is known as the Dirt Diva on the River Radio, 94.9 FM, in Boise, Idaho. Her articles on gardening have been published in numerous publications including *MaryJane's Farm*, *Fine Gardening*, *American Gardener*, and *Leaf*. An accomplished horticulturalist and garden designer, Mary Ann has designed public, private, and commercial gardens. With John Cretti, she coauthored *The Rocky Mountain Gardener's Handbook* (2012). She lives and gardens in Boise and loves traveling throughout the western United States. Follow her escapades on her website, gardensofthewildwildwest.com.